# Language Redeemed:
Chaucer's Mature Poetry

LANGUAGE REDEEMED:

CHAUCER'S MATURE POETRY

David Williams

Sapientia Press
of Ave Maria University

Sapientia Press
of Ave Maria University
1025 Commons Circle
Naples, FL 34119
888-343-8607

Cover Image: The murder of St. Thomas Becket, ca. 1500–1550. © British Library/HIP/Art Resource, NY.

Photo Credit: HIP/Art Resource, NY

Cover Design: Eloise Anagnost

Printed in the United States of America.

Library of Congress Control Number: 2006939256

ISBN-10: 1-932589-35-X

ISBN-13: 978-1-932589-35-1

For Mary Smith Podles and Leon Podles

Magnanimity is the crown of all the virtues

— Aristotle, *Nichomachean Ethics* (IV, 3 1124)

TABLE OF CONTENTS

 INTRODUCTION

REALISM AND NOMINALISM

In verbis verum amare, non verba
—*De Doctrina Christiana* IV, XI, 26

ECLARING THAT "in words it is the truth we love, not the words," St. Augustine expressed in a full and economical way the essence of Christian Realism, a philosophical view in which words are seen as openings to truths independent of the words themselves. Of course, the love of words and their truth is nowhere more ardent than in the heart of the poet whose very profession is words, and so it is not surprising that we often find in the writing of poets a meditation on the nature of language itself. The most outstanding modern example would be, perhaps, T. S. Eliot, whose theoretical considerations of poetry assume the character of a philosophy of language. An ancient example of this poet–philosopher function is the man whom Eliot venerated so deeply, Dante Alighieri. Both men, profoundly influenced by St. Augustine, would heartily agree that "in words it is the truth we love." Between the two of them stands Geoffrey Chaucer who lived in exactly the time in the history of philosophy when Christian Realism was most seriously challenged and most vigorously defended, and it should come as no surprise that a poet as philosophical as Chaucer would enter the debate.

The Middle Ages inherited from their Platonic and Neo-Platonic past the view that so-called "universals"—things such as Justice, Human Nature, the Good—possessed a form of being that, indeed, they existed in some way, independent of human knowledge of them and of the words we use to signify them. Thus, for the Realist, the universal is prior to the particular: What is beautiful is so through participation in the universal—Beauty; human beings share a common nature because they are the individual manifestations of the universal—Humanity. In this sense, a highly Neo-Platonic one, all things in the world are real in and of themselves, and are, as well, signs of a higher reality in which they participate. Thus the world of the Realist is a thoroughly symbolic one and of particular appeal to the poet.

The challenge to this view began around the twelfth century with what came to be known as Nominalism; its most famous proponent was the early fourteenth-century Franciscan logician William of Ockham. Although there are as many variations of Nominalism as there are of Realism, in general Nominalists hold that universals are nothing more than general terms used to indicate mental concepts. Human experience of similar individual things, such as our encounter with other human beings, allows us to have a general conception of these individuals and to give a common name to that conception—"Humanity." This idea that the name, or word, is the extent of the reality of the universal gives this school its name: "Nominalism" from the Latin *nomen*, "name." What is key to the Nominalist view is that only individuals really exist; particulars precede universals and give meaning to them, and, further, universals are mere mental realities—words—not ontological phenomena like the things they name.

Both schools can be said to take their origins from different answers to questions posed in a fundamental philosophical text of the Middle Ages, Porphyry's *Isagoge*, a student's introduction to Aristotle's *Categories*, in which the third-century philosopher raises certain questions about universals, which, given the introductory nature of his text, he declares he will not try to answer. The questions, however, provoked plenty of answers from others. Porphyry asks whether universals are real or merely words; if real, is the universal corporeal or incorporeal; does the universal exist independently or correlative with and dependent upon the particular?[1] Various answers to these questions determine whether one is a Realist, a Moderate Realist, a Nominalist, or an Extreme Nominalist.

The great French scholar Etienne Gilson, whose work on the history of mediaeval philosophy is considered fundamental, begins the story of the mediaeval controversy concerning Realism and Nominalism with the brilliant twelfth-century logician Peter Abelard. According to Gilson, Abelard considers the question of universals using the wrong philosophical method, and this error, repeated and deepened by Nominalists over the next two centuries, ends in the dissolution of mediaeval philosophy. The error was that Abelard used logic to discuss a question that was beyond the powers of logic to solve:

> He, therefore, quietly proceeded to discuss the philosophical questions (posed by Porphyry) as if he were still standing on logical ground. Now it was legitimate for Abailard to ask, in his own words, "how the universal definition can be applied to things"; but logic is not directly concerned with such problems.[2]

Long before Abelard, Boethius, one of the early founders of mediaeval thought, had tackled Porphyry's questions; in fact he both translated the *Isagoge,* and wrote two commentaries on it. This sixth-century thinker showed himself to be a Moderate Realist through his opinion that the universal is embodied in the particular; for Boethius, the universal is something that really exists, and the particular is the material expression of it.[3]

---

[1] Porphyry uses the terms *genera* and *species.* See Porphyry the Phoenician, *Isagoge,* trans., introduction, and notes Edward W. Warren. Toronto: Pontifical Institute of Mediaeval Studies. *Mediaeval Studies in Translation* (1975): 27.

[2] Etienne Gilson, *The Unity of Philosophical Experience* (New York: Scribner and Sons, 1937), 11.

[3] Considered as a whole, Boethius's position is, in fact, closer to Aristotle's and St. Thomas's in that he considers the universal as really existing, but coexistent

Geoffrey Chaucer, widely recognized as a philosophical poet, engaged the debate concerning Realism and Nominalism in his writings, especially his later poetry, as a means of constructing many of his characters—there are Nominalists and Realists scattered all over Chaucer's writings—and to create the settings of his narratives in which, true to his philosophical bent, he addresses fundamental questions of human existence. Boethius's position on the Realist–Nominalist controversy is important in a discussion of Chaucer's use of the debate in his poetry, since Chaucer was sufficiently impressed with Boethianism that he devoted a significant amount of his time to translating Boethius's *Consolation of Philosophy*, a basic source in mediaeval philosophy and a prime expression of mediaeval Realism.

The pertinence of the Realist–Nominalist controversy to poetry has to do, on the one hand, with the relation of words to the real, and on the other, the efficacy of symbolic representation. In its extreme form, Nominalism reduces reality to isolated individuals and their particular experiences of the world, related, if at all, not by anything inherent in themselves or the things experienced, but by words alone. By both philosophical and psychological extension, this tends toward the reduction of reality to words. Although words are the currency of poets, their value consists in their ability to give unity to human experience by relating that experience to truths that they represent and that they make present in the poem. As the distinguished Ockham scholar Gordon Leff has pointed out, Nominalism's stance that the individual human experience of the particular is all that is "real," inevitably slides into a form of psychologism.[4] While psychology is, perhaps congenial to the novel, a form yet to

---

with the particular. This is the position of the Moderate Realist. Plato is normally considered an "Extreme" Realist, believing the Universal to be completely independent of and prior to the particular.

[4] Gordon Leff, *Medieval Thought: Saint Augustine to Ockham* (Chicago: Quadrangle Books, 1958), 284ff.

be created in the Middle Ages, it is entirely inadequate to the poetic vision, one that is in one way or another always anagogical.

Realism, on the other hand, with its emphasis on the existential reality of our abstract conceptions, views the things of this world as meaningful signs of truths that make sense of our existence. It is a common mistake, especially among literary scholars, to accuse realism of diminishing the value of this world, the here and now, and the human experience of it, by aggrandizing the value of the abstract "Other World." However, the genius of the mediaeval Catholic rendering of Neo-Platonic Realism is that it does just the opposite: The world and all the things in it are of inestimable value exactly because, created by a loving God, they participate in the paradigmatic universals by which He created all that is. Theology and philosophy can communicate this perception to our intellects, but poetry and liturgy incarnate it as a reality in our hearts and minds. It was to do just this that T. S. Eliot wrote poetry, that Dante wrote poetry, and, as I will try to show, that Chaucer wrote poetry.

In contemporary discussions of this subject, especially perhaps, in Chaucer studies, it is often asserted that whereas Nominalism recognizes the contingency of human knowledge and the anthropomorphic dimension of human predication, Realism boldly claims the possibility of univocal knowledge of things through the use of human intellect.[5] Witness, they say, the torturous efforts of Scholasticism to create intellectual proofs of the existence of God; look, in contrast, at the humility with which the mediaeval Nominalist admits that faith alone provides our understanding of God. This view, somewhat caricatured here, is quite inaccurate. No Christian thinker of the Middle Ages or any other time has ever asserted that the human intellect can adequate the Real, let alone

---

[5] For a full discussions of such "misunderstandings," see Robert Myles, *Chaucerian Realism* (Cambridge: D. S. Brewer, 1994), 1–21. Myles's work is generally considered the best close study of Nominalism and Realism in the context of Chaucer's poetry.

comprehend—that is, *contain*—God. We need only bring to mind Dionysius the Areopagite, a thorough-going Extreme Realist, and his urgent warnings against the arrogance of the human intellect in its attempts to know and to limit God to the names we give Him[6] to understand that every Realist, as well as every Nominalist, in the Middle Ages adopted the same view on this subject. Thomas Aquinas, whom we might consider the archetype Scholastic philosopher, quotes Dionysius in his work more often than any other source except Aristotle, and, although his own Realism is of the moderate kind, Thomas heartily agrees with the Areopagite that the human intellect can never know God as God truly is.

There are, of course, differences between the Nominalist and the Realist in epistemological matters: The Realist conceives of the human intellect as a God-given tool intended to be used to investigate the created world to the fullest extent of its capacities and, by the study of individual things, gain some knowledge of their universal origins. The motto of St. Anselm sums up the spirit of the Realist intellectual pursuit: *Fides quaerens intellectum* (faith seeking understanding).[7] Nominalism limits the intellectually knowable to the phenomena of human sense experience and ideas about that experience. Belief in God is warehoused, we might say, in the concept of "faith," which Nominalists segregated from knowledge as a way of dealing with what Nominalism cannot explain. As history demonstrates, it was not long before faith, and God as well, were exiled altogether from mainstream western philosophy. Mediaeval Nominalism eventually came to emphasize

---

6 "We must not dare to resort to words or conceptions concerning the hidden divinity which transcends being, apart from what the sacred scriptures have divinely revealed. Since the unknowing of what is beyond being is something above and beyond speech, mind, or being itself, one should ascribe to it an understanding beyond being." *Divine Names,* I, 588a, *and passim,* in *Pseudo-Dionysius: The Complete Works,* trans. Colm Luibheid; foreword and notes, Paul Rorem; preface, René Roques; Introductions, Jarolslave Pelikan et al. (New York: Paulist Press, 1987), 49.

7 Anselm, *Proslogion,* 947.

the contingency of human knowledge to the point of anticipating the relativism of later periods, in the sense that, if human understanding is based on individual experience, and if there is no inherent bond between one person's experience and another's (that is, there is nothing real that they, as knowers, share, like human nature; nor is there anything universal or essential to be perceived in the thing known), then one person's perception of the truth is as good and as "true" as another's.

As such a view settles in, the very concept of Truth becomes questionable: If there are many valid versions of the truth, then there is no one truth; if there is no one truth, there is no Truth, per se, at all. The progression is from Nominalism to Relativism to Nihilism. This, of course, is where we find ourselves today in mainstream western thought. Although the origins of this development are in the Middle Ages, the philosophical spirit of Chaucer's times is much more diverse than our own, and while the universities were being rapidly taken over by the Nominalist *moderni*, the Realist tradition was being kept alive to a great extent by the poets.

GEOFFREY CHAUCER: POETIC REALIST

GEOFFREY CHAUCER was a poet of the English royal court and remained in favor through the reigns of three kings of England. Born around 1342 to a wealthy merchant family, Chaucer served in his adolescent years as a page to the Countess of Ulster, daughter-in-law of King Edward III, and, when Edward was succeeded by his grandson, Richard II, Chaucer continued to receive royal largesse. Chaucer's good fortunes were due largely to the fact that he was the protégé of the most powerful man in England, John of Gaunt, whose son, Henry Bolingbroke, eventually deposed Richard II and became King Henry IV. Under Henry, Chaucer continued in royal favor.

In addition to his poetry, Chaucer devoted himself to translation. One of his earliest works was the translation of the *Roman de la Rose*, a Neo-Platonic allegorical poem of the twelfth century. Later, around 1380, he produced his monumental translation of Boethius's great work, *De Consolatione Philosophiae,* titled in English the *Consolation of Philosophy.* Chaucer's early literary compositions include *The Book of the Duchess*, written as a consolation for his patron on the occasion of the death of Blanche, Duchess of Lancaster, John of Gaunt's wife. In the next decade, 1372–1382, he wrote the *Parliament of Fowls*, the *House of Fame*, and, sometime before 1385, *Troilus and Criseyde*. Several of the stories that he used in his last work, the *Canterbury Tales*, were written in this period as well.

Like other poets of his time, Chaucer wrote as an avocation while earning his living in a variety of ways, several of which, we might imagine, may well have furnished him with material for his poetry. It is supposed that it was as a royal envoy to the Continent that Chaucer became familiar with the elegant poetry of France and the grand long narratives of Italy. It is thought that he could read Latin, French, Norman, and Italian (something not uncommon among the educated of the fourteenth century). Chaucer also served as comptroller of customs for the Port of London, a post of great economic importance. In 1385 he became justice of the peace for the county of Kent, and the next year he was elected Member of Parliament. When he died on October 25, 1400, leaving his masterpiece, the *Canterbury Tales* unfinished, he was eminent enough to be buried in Westminster Abbey: He was the first to occupy what became known as Poets' Corner, where today his neighbors include such eminences as Dryden, Tennyson, Browning, and Dickens.

In terms of the narratives that Chaucer worked with in his later poetry, the principle influence is clearly the wonderful Italian storyteller Giovanni Boccaccio, whose *Il Filostrato* provided the general outline of Chaucer's *Troilus and Criseyde* and whose *Decamerone*, a collection of tales told by aristocrats fleeing the malaria, gave Chaucer the idea of the pilgrimage "frame-tale" structure of the *Canterbury Tales*.[1] However, for the conceptual and philosophical influences on Chaucer's thinking and work, for what we may call the poet's "worldview," we must look to another Italian genius— Dante. The greatest poet of the mediaeval world (if not of all time), he presented Chaucer with a stunning example of the poetic use of the noblest philosophical and theological ideas of the time, which

---

[1] All citations of Chaucer's works are from *The Riverside Chaucer*, ed. Larry Benson (Boston: Houghton Mifflin, 2000). Modern transliterations of the Middle English are my own.

became the essence of the English poet's mature writing. Behind these mediaeval sources, and through them, the great classical writers of antiquity made their mark on Chaucer as he himself makes clear when he consigns his *Troilus and Criseyde* to the tradition of Virgil, Ovid, Homer, Lucan, and Statius (*Troilus and Criseyde* [*TC*] V, 1790–93). Chaucer's own Christian tradition and education provided him with two more fundamental influences on his thinking and his writing—Boethius and St. Augustine.

Chaucer was eclectic in an age when originality as we know it was far from the most valued quality in creative writing. Rather, the sensibilities of the Middle Ages seem to have responded best to the classical criterion of traditional stories retold in creative ways. Thus, *Troilus and Criseyde* is an epic romance that is the retelling of the single most recounted story of the Middle Ages, the fall of Troy, as Chaucer found it in Boccaccio. But Boccaccio had found it in Guido delle Colonne's *Historia Trojana*, which, itself had been derived from the French poet Benoit de Sainte-Maure's *Roman de Troye*. Each rendition changed its source to a greater or lesser degree, but it is indisputable that in Chaucer's hands the story is altered in the most brilliant manner.

As with the *Troilus*, so in the *Canterbury Tales*, none of the stories that constitute the work are original with Chaucer. Instead, whether the tale is taken from Petrarch or Boccaccio or folklore, Chaucer retells it in a way that draws out its aesthetic potential and expands its philosophical implications. In his early work, such as the *Parliament of Fowls* and *House of Fame*, there appear signs of a variety of narrative techniques that Chaucer develops with successive writings until, in the *Troilus*, they reach their penultimate form, and, in the *Canterbury Tales*, their fullness. Two of the most important of these are (1) the "naïve-narrator" device, in which, through the manipulations of a hidden author, the audience understands more than the narrator tells them, and (2) the "story-within-a story," or "frame-tale," structure, which consists of a series of stories unified by the context in which they are told. Still another is what we might call the "slip-of-the-tongue" device, in which a character says more than he or she intended to say and thereby reveals aspects of themselves or their subject that they would have preferred remain hidden.

We will examine Chaucer's use of these devices in his late poems, *Troilus and Criseyde* and *Canterbury Tales*, in order to see how the poet explores a variety of philosophical questions and even contributes to their answers, not through a philosophical, dialectical discourse, but through poetic imagination.

TROILUS AND CRISEYDE

1 **Troilus and Criseyde**

BOOK ONE

THE MEDIAEVALS cherished the idea that they were descendents of the survivors of Troy, a notion derived principally from Virgil's *Aeneid* in which the virtuous Trojan, Aeneas, founds Rome, and his descendent, Felix Brutus, founds Britain. Thus the story of the fall of Troy and its aftermath became the myth of origins for the Europeans, and this accounts for the popularity of the narrative. So fervently embraced was this legend that in Chaucer's time the English Parliament entertained the idea of changing the name of London to Troynovant (New Troy).

Whereas Virgil's narrative is panoramic, Chaucer's, like its immediate sources, focuses on a minor incident concerning minor characters in the Trojan epic and makes of them the center of the work. Thus the potential of a microcosm–macrocosm structure is set up in which the fall of Troy is mirrored in the moral "fall" of the main characters. Troilus, whose name, "little Troy," bespeaks this idea, is the youngest son of Priam, King of Troy, and, in Virgil, a figure of much less importance than his brothers. He is, however, made the center of Chaucer's piece when he falls in love with Criseyde, a figure again of less than minor importance in the ancient sources. Although Briseida, as Boccaccio named her, is central in the Italian tale, she is seen to be less and less important as one traces her back in earlier versions. Similarly, whereas Chaucer superbly rendered the character of Pandarus, Criseyde's uncle and Troilus's procurer, Boccaccio's Pandaro is far less developed and still less so in Boccaccio's sources.

Chaucer's 8,000-line romance epic is structured in five books, each begun with introductory stanzas, designated in the middle three books as the *Prohemium*, spoken in an ambiguous voice as a means of distinguishing the Narrator from the Author. Instead of beginning the story at once, the introductory stanzas of the first book introduce the Narrator, in which he describes his intentions as storyteller and the methods he will use. These stanzas put the alert reader on guard as to the nature of the Narrator because of the strangeness of his self-portrait:

> I who serve servants of the God of love,
> I dare not to love, awkward as I am. (*TC* I, 15–16)

Here we have a Narrator so distanced from his subject and from his characters that he cannot "feel" what they feel and so, as he claims a few lines later (*TC* I, 47–51), he is satisfied to pray for lovers and record their story "*As if* I were their own dear brother" (*TC* I, 52, my emphasis). This prepares us for the Narrator's further claim that he is a mere "translator" of his sources.

The principal figures of the first 56 lines are the Narrator and the audience itself, for in the very first stanza, the Narrator declares that to describe the sorrows of Troilus, "My purpose is, before I part from *you* (*TC* I, 5, my emphasis). This personalizing of the audience reminds us that Chaucer may have actually been reading his poem to a live audience of the royal court, and that what we have here is his opening address to them. If that is so, the real author's adoption of a fictional narrative voice is even more humorous and ironic, since there loom two poetic voices, that of Chaucer-Author and that of Chaucer-Narrator, and the potential for conflict and comic confusion between them is considerable. We soon hear the distinction between the voices and the conflict begins to emerge through the device of undermining the audience's confidence in Chaucer-Narrator by his frequent interruptions of the narrative in order to explain his dubious literary principles and methods, his reliance on equally dubious sources, and, above all, his lack of poetic emotion.

The story begins with a one-stanza summary of the background to the Trojan war—Paris's "ravishing" of Helen—and zeros in on Calkas, a pagan priest and seer and father of our heroine, Criseyde:

> It so happened that in this town there was
> Living a lord of great authority,
> A grand, true seer whose name was Calkas
> That in divining was so good that he
> Knew for sure that Troy would all destroyed be. (*TC* I, 64–68)

This stanza, introducing a minor character who does not reappear until the end of the story, is of considerable importance, not only because it establishes the psycho-moral setting in which Criseyde is presented—her father a traitor, she abandoned—but because it also creates a poetic image of a profound philosophical problem: Calkas knows correctly that in the future Troy will be destroyed. Is Troy destroyed *because* Calkas's foreknowledge is true?

This is the fictional presentation of the central question in the mediaeval debate over predestination and free will: If God is omniscient, then He knows—in addition to all other things— whether or not I will be saved or damned. Since God's knowledge must be correct, does it not follow that I (and all others) are already predestined? If so, how then can we conceive of human beings having free will? Answers to these questions not only constitute much of mediaeval philosophy but have profoundly shaped western culture, particularly religious culture and theology.

In a brilliant conceit, Chaucer leads us to an answer through poetic structure. Our poet's favorite philosopher, Boethius, had provided a thoroughly Realist answer to this problem by conceiving

God as resident in a "lofty tower" from which He has a perspective upon all time. We can imagine a man in a tower looking down upon a crossroads and seeing two charioteers each on separate roads traveling toward the intersection. He perceives that the two vehicles are traveling at the same speed and that they are equidistant to the intersection. He knows they will collide. They do collide. Did his correct foreknowledge *cause* the collision?[1]

In the Boethian allegory, the man in the tower is God residing in eternity looking down on the span of human time, seeing there all the events that have occurred, are occurring, will occur within that span as if they were happening in a present moment, just as God's "time" is an eternal "now."

In adapting this conceit, Chaucer, we may say, does Boethius one better. He puts his audience in the tower. In the construct of Chaucer's poem, we, the audience, enter into a present narrative about our own past. Historically the siege and fall of Troy is an accomplished event in time, but poetically we are in the fiction of it happening "before our eyes," as it were. Thus when Chaucer tells us that Calkas knew that Troy would fall, we know that Calkas is right. Within the fiction, we must ask: Will Troy then fall because of *our* correct knowledge that it will fall? Within history we must ask, *did* Troy fall because of our knowledge that it *did* fall? This last even more absurd possibility forces us to answer in the negative and to recognize that foreknowledge is not a cause and that the events in this world are independent of human knowing.

Chaucer has so manipulated the Boethian figure that we, the audience, become the one in the tower watching Calkas knowing something about the future in the fictional present that is already accomplished in our historical past. Furthermore, by the same analogy that Boethius first used, Chaucer makes us God-like in the glimpse he gives us of eternity, a perspective in which past, present, and future are one.

---

[1] See Chaucer's translation of the *Consolation* (V, prosa 6) in the *Riverside Chaucer*.

Whereas this allusion, used early in the poem, gives us an idea of the work's philosophical direction, it also prefigures the development of a deeply religious worldview. Human nature, the nature of time, the human existential predicament, the nature and extent of free will, all topical concerns of mediaeval philosophy, are inseparable from theological questions about the nature of eternity, God's omnipotence, man's knowledge of God, and divine Providence, and both discourses are meditated upon in Chaucer's poetry.

This is why Chaucer does not open the poem by presenting Criseyde herself, but rather by giving us the context in which, as a moral agent, she will exercise her free will. Criseyde awakes one morning to find herself the daughter of a traitor against whom her fellow Trojans want to take vengeance, although she is innocent of any fault. This, we might say, is her destiny: None of us determine completely the situations in which we find ourselves; they are largely determined for us. But as Chaucer's narrative demonstrates, how Criseyde acts within her externally determined context is a matter of Criseyde's own free choices, and, of course, at the tropological, or didactic, level of the text, so are ours.

Chaucer-Narrator boldly declares Criseyde the most beautiful woman in Troy and, at the same time, the least courageous: She was "almost out of her mind for fear and dread" (*TC* I, 108); we are reminded throughout the story of Criseyde's profound insecurity, to the point that she suggests the allegorical figure, Timor: "She was the fearfullest being who ever lived" (*TC* II, 450), but also: "Criseyde was this lady's name, indeed, / The fairest woman in all Troy, I deem" (*TC* I, 99–100). Here, however, our suspicion about the Narrator deepens. Doesn't he know, as the rest of the world does, who the most beautiful woman in Troy and all the world is? This device both undermines the Narrator's authority and simultaneously associates Criseyde with Helen who had a distinctly unsavory reputation in the Middle Ages.

As a widow and an abandoned daughter, Criseyde lacks male protection, so she throws herself on the mercy of Hector, eldest son of

King Priam. It is not surprising that as one of the most revered characters of the mediaeval legend, Hector gives Criseyde the morally
sound advice that allows her to "behave in such manner that her
honor / Was clear to all, and while she lived in Troy / Her mien was
so proper that she was loved / and respected by everybody" (*TC* I,
127–30). That is to say, Criseyde developed what Boethius's Lady
Philosophy recommends in the *Consolation of Philosophy*, the "inner
life," the source of true security and true autonomy.

Troilus is introduced as an immature, arrogant youth who dis-
parages the idea of romantic commitment until he is "hit" with the
image of Criseyde whom he perceives in a pagan temple, an
important associative detail, since it hints at the poetic paradigms
that Chaucer is using: Petrarch first lays eyes on Laura in a church;
Dante, as well, first encounters Beatrice in a church; and there are
numerous other examples of the meeting of the beloved in a temple or church.[2] Whereas such encounters lead both Petrarch and
Dante to pure loves and poetic inspiration, "love at first sight"
drives Troilus into a maddening passion that Chaucer describes in
medical terms as a disease, and the vocabulary depicting Troilus's
love is marked throughout by words for sickness and death: "Suddenly he felt as if he were dying" (*TC* I, 306); "O living death, O
sweet hurt so strange," (*TC* I, 411); "By God I wish I were at the
door of / Death arrived" (*TC* I, 525–26).

The Narrator describes Troilus's malaise in the "Canticus Troili,"
a song the youth sings that, our Narrator tells us, he is reporting in
even greater detail than he finds in his source, Lollius, by rehearsing
every word that Troilus actually sang. More absurd than this
claim—to know more than his source provides—is the identification of the source itself. As far as is known, there never was a Lol-

---

[2] In the case of Petrarch and Dante, the encounter with the beloved leads to
poetic and spiritual inspiration. But there is a negative use of the convention
of encounters in a sacred place as we see in the tradition that Paris first met
Helen in a temple.

lius, and it is generally thought that Chaucer intended this error on the part of the Narrator to further undermine him.

Troilus, the Warrior, is discovered in bed moaning and groaning by his best friend, Pandarus, third of the three principle characters in the poem. Chaucer found the model for this character in Boccaccio's Pandaro but made extensive changes to him, and these changes are significant. Pandaro is, indeed, Troilo's friend and, as ideal friendship was conceived, they are the same age; in the model, Pandaro is Criseyde's cousin, whereas Chaucer makes him her uncle, suggesting that he is older than Criseyde who is herself thought to be older than Troilus. This makes Pandarus considerably older than Troilus, and, therefore, an inappropriate friend according to the classical and mediaeval theories of friendship, which stressed equality in all things, including age, between friends.[3] These changes also make Pandarus Criseyde's closest male relative, and he is therefore responsible for protecting her interests.

Pandarus's most outstanding characteristic is his astounding ability with words. Chaucer has made of Pandarus a character who truly loves words but not truth, for in his worldview there is no truth. From the moment of his appearance, Pandarus's discursive power drives the narrative, and it seems that he gradually usurps the role of the Narrator in steering the plot toward a dénouement that the Narrator would eschew. Like Humpty Dumpty, his nineteenth-century descendent, Pandarus believes that "a word . . . means just what I choose it to mean,"[4] a creed as opposed to Augustinian Realism as might be conceived.

Pandarus's primary concern in discovering Troilus in distress is to know the object of his passion, and, when traditional methods—such as rousing the friend to anger through insults—fail, he resorts

---

[3] There were many treatises on friendship known in the Middle Ages. One of the most influential ones was *Cicero on Old Age and On Friendship*, trans. and introduction Frank O. Copley (Ann Arbor, MI: University of Michigan Press, 1967).

[4] Lewis Carroll, *Through the Looking Glass,* chapter VI.

to what he is best at: sophistry. Indeed, in Pandarus Chaucer creates a stunning portrait of the contemporary fourteenth-century Sophist, who, like his classical ancestors, believes that the ethical is a linguistic construct, that universal ideals love and friendship, for instance—have no reality beyond the words we use for them.

Playing on Troilus's respect for their friendship, Pandarus begins an assault on his friend's privacy in order, as he tells him, "to share with you all your pain" (*TC* I, 589). This "sharing," as we increasingly perceive, is to include more than Troilus's "pain," for, in bringing the youth to the indulgence of his desire, Pandarus intends to share, however vicariously, Troilus's pleasure, as well.

Troilus initially resists Pandarus's offer that his "advice may well help *us*" (*TC* I, 620, my emphasis), even revealing more than he himself can understand: "You, who never scored in the game of love, / How the hell can you get me to heaven?" (*TC* I, 622–23). It will be precisely by making a heaven of the hell of disordered desire and a hell of the heaven of true love—by having the metaphoric word "hell" mean "heaven"—that Pandarus will manipulate both Troilus and Criseyde.

But, there is more. What are we to make of Troilus's revelation that Pandarus himself has never succeeded in gratifying his desires? The idea that Pandarus is a failure in the very thing in which he claims to be an expert advisor is reinforced in various ways throughout the poem. When, for instance, Criseyde playfully asks her uncle, "Where do you fit in the dance of love?" Pandarus answers, "By God, . . . I always hop along behind!" (*TC* II, 1106–7). That the *dance* of love was a risqué mediaeval reference to the sex act seems to hint at something rather alarming in Pandarus's reply and in his psychology.

It is, in fact, in this persona, and a few others, that we see Chaucer's extraordinary ability to delineate character in psychological terms, an aspect of fiction not much developed in the Middle Ages. From the *Canterbury Tales*, the Wyf of Bath is often cited as one example of a psychologically realistic character. However, the one best suited to a comparison with Pandarus is the Pardoner, whose defining characteristics are his way with words and his sexual impotence.[5] While Pandarus's perverse involvement in Troilus's sexuality may indeed be given a psychological motive, it is, as with Chaucer's other psychological depictions, also symbolic. Like the ancient Sophist and the fourteenth-century Nominalist as well, Pandarus conceives of words as having behind them no objective, transcendent meaning, but only the signifying power assigned by human experience. It is, at best, an anemic sense of words as signs that lack seminal power to incarnate the Real.

Thus, Pandarus's sexual impotence signifies the impotence of his Nomiinalist worldview. His parasitic need to osmose with Troilus's youthful, manly vigor bespeaks an absence that is first psychological, but then intellectual, and ultimately spiritual. It is interesting that among Troilus's several shortcomings are his linguistic and literary incompetence: He is not good with words; he doesn't know or like "old stories," and he is so severely handicapped rhetorically that Pandarus has to teach him how to write a love letter. Poor Troilus thinks that words are simple and mean what they say, and this naïveté, exploited by Pandarus, is his downfall. It would almost seem that, put together—the youth's eros with the elder's intellect—Troilus and Pandarus would make a whole man.[6]

Pandarus's verbal assault on Troilus intensifies when the young man demurs from revealing the name of the woman who has so deeply affected him. In a series of sophistical analogies Pandarus reveals more of himself than he would ever have consciously intended, or than Troilus can understand. In answer to Troilus's

---

[5] E. Talbot Donaldson makes a similar comparison in "Chaucer's Three P's: Pandarus, Pardoner, and Poet," *Michigan Quarterly Review* 14 (1975): 282–301.

[6] This relation of the older man who has to supply the words of love to express the young man's passion seems to be a recurring literary topos in which the object of desire, the woman, falls in love as much with the words as the man. The most interesting modern example is Rostand's *Cyrano de Bergerac.*

objection that he has not been able himself to succeed in love, Pandarus responds:

> I have myself seen a blind man pass safe
> Where a man with eyesight did fall aside.
> And thus a fool may well a wise man guide. (*TC* I, 628–30)

The inappropriateness of this analogy is clear to all but Troilus. Pandarus is in no way "blind" nor Troilus "clear sighted." Pandarus has already called Troilus a fool (*TC* I, 618) and will do so often throughout the poem. To identify the simple, ignorant youth now as a wise man and himself as a fool is to deceptively and mockingly invert the real situation. Pandarus continues:

> A whetstone is no carving instrument,
> And yet it sharpens well the tools that carve.
> So where you see that I have gone astray,
> Avoid that error—that's just common sense.
> And thus are wise men often warned by fools.
> If you are so warned, the better for you.
> By its contrary is everything revealed. (*TC* I, 631–37)

In comparing himself to a whetstone that sharpens tools for cutting, Pandarus inadvertently reveals something of the psychology of his relationship to Troilus: He will "sharpen" the youth's appetite in order to make up for his lack of one, and in so doing derive some vicarious enjoyment.[7]

The last line of this stanza is, I would suggest, the single most important in the poem because it provides the basic concept of the work and the key to its structure and meaning: contrariety. Today

---

[7] These sophistical analogies continue throughout the first part of Book I: "How could one know sweetness without tasting bitterness?" (I, 638–39). With this analogy, taken from Boethius, Pandarus tries to persuade Troilus that bitterness is good, or more generally, that the negative is as good as the positive; "I am to you as Oenone was to Paris" (I, 652–65). Here Pandarus compares himself to a jealous nymph and Troilus to his narcissistic brother. And so on.

in epistemology and philosophy of language, as in their equivalent in the Middle Ages, it is understood that contrariety and opposition are principle factors in meaning and understanding. It is, in fact, difference that makes words and concepts meaningful—the contrast between the sound "m" and the sound "e" that allows the word "me" to signify; the concept of justice understood by its difference from injustice. But it is only where similitude inheres that dissimilitude, or difference, can be significant. In Chaucer's adaptation of this philosophical principle, the audience is prompted to extend Pandarus's aphorism and ask, if everything is revealed by its contrary, does Pandarus have a contrary? Who is Troilus's opposite? Who Criseyde's? What is the opposite of this poem we are reading and trying to understand? These are questions that are easier to answer by the end of the poem.

Discovering that the object of Troilus's passion is none other than his own niece, Pandarus is delighted and assures Troilus that it will be a simple matter to get Criseyde for him. Belittling Troilus's scruples about being honorable and decent in the affair ("that's what they all say"; *TC* I, 1038), Pandarus sets out in Book II to begin his siege of Criseyde. Here, at the same time, Pandarus begins to compete with the Narrator in a struggle to control the plot and create a narrative that both reflects and satisfies his cupidity.

2 Troilus and Criseyde

Book Two

THE *PROHEMIUM* TO BOOK II contains several hints as to Chaucer's poetic intention in *Troilus and Criseyde*, as well as a demonstration of the complicated use of voice. There seem, in fact, to be two voices speaking alternately, that of the historical poet and that of the fictional narrator. Chaucer-Author begins:

> Out of these black waves to sail, O wind,
> O wind, the weather now begins to clear;
> For in this sea the ship of my talent
> Has such labour that uneasy I steer.
> This "sea" I call the tempestuous tale
> Of sorrow and despair that Troilus felt. (*TC* II, 1–6)

Here we have a clear echo of the *Commedia* and thus, perhaps, a hint as to the dynamic of contrariety:

> To sail the better waters, hoist the sails
> Of the little ship of my talent
> And leave behind these cruel, dark seas.[1]

---

[1] Dante Alighieri, *Divina Commedia*. 3 vols. (Milan: Rizzoli, 1949). *Purgatorio* I, 1–3. All citations are from this edition and all translations to English are my own.

In Book I the Narrator revealed his source as the spurious Lollius. Here Chaucer-Author reveals his true source as Dante by using the Italian's opening lines of the *Purgatorio*. In so doing, Chaucer creates a paradigm for his entire project: the use of sets of conflicting sources, one set made up of references that are not true sources for the poem; the other made up of the genuine, but concealed, sources. Such a device, once noticed, begins to clarify and expand the principle that "by its contrary is everything revealed."

In the second stanza of the *Prohemium* the voice shifts, and it is once again our Narrator who speaks:

> O Lady mine, O Cleo, be ye
> My spark, be ye my muse to rhyme this book
> 'Til it be done. No other art need I!
> And I ask all lovers to excuse the
> Lack of passion in my poem, for not
> From feeling, but from Latin I translate. (*TC* II, 8–13)

Here the gradual undermining of the Narrator's credibility advances. Clio, as muse of history, is hardly the appropriate muse to aid in rhyming. Melpomene or even Polyhymnia would be possible candidates, but the most likely would be Calliope, muse of epic poetry and the one Dante invokes just after he has used the metaphor of the "little ship." This use of Dante followed by a misuse of Dante is meant to distinguish, we may believe, the voice of Chaucer-Author from the voice of Chaucer-Narrator. Further, his insistence on his lack of poetic sentiment and on his role as mere translator distinguishes him from Chaucer and, for that matter, any other genuine poet writing of love.

Chaucer-Author returns in the fourth stanza to present the reader with a surprising little theory of language in the context of speaking of love:

> And well you know that forms of language change
> Within a thousand years, and words that then

Signified now don't. Yet they were used and,
Truly meant the same love as we do now.
. . . .
In the end, you know, all roads lead to Rome.
   (*TC* II, 22–25, 36)

As a philosophical comment on the nature of language, these lines clearly put forth a Realist perspective. Love, Chaucer is telling us, is universal, and the human experience of it particular, varying from culture to culture, but recognizable through the participation of each love in the universal. Just as the Trojans felt the joys and sorrows of love and represented those feelings with Greek words, so too the English have the same experience, but use English words to express it. The signifiers are various and particular, but the signified is universal; the reality is objective, its sign relative.

Such a declaration not only reinforces the Realist worldview of the poem, it also authorizes a certain degree of allegory in its reading. If Love is a universal, than Troilus and Criseyde's experience of it is comparable to mine and yours and that compatibility is the foundation for our "sympathy" with the characters. Further, in Troilus's and Criseyde's successes and failures in love we glimpse our own, and therein lies the foundation of the didactic level of the poem.

In Book II Pandarus sets out to seduce Criseyde for his friend Troilus. This project is contextualized in a deeply menacing way that gives a strong negative charge to the nature of Pandarus's visit to his niece:

In Spring, when Phoebus does his bright beams spread
   In the white bull, on the third day of May,
It happened that, as I shall you recount,
   This Pandarus, for all his crafty speech,
Well felt his own share of titillation. (*TC* II, 54–58)
. . . .
He himself fell a bit in love that day
And to bed he went in agitation. (*TC* II, 62–63)

Chaucer is explicit here that Pandarus derives vicarious erotic excitement from Troilus's passion and his own involvement in it as go-between. Moreover, the poet's choice of rhetorical allusion to the white bull suggests a certain violence in the sexuality that is the center of the description and the object of Pandarus's visit to Criseyde. The myth and widespread artistic theme of the Rape of Europa features Zeus adopting the form of a white bull to lure and rape the maiden Europa. The reference here is exacerbated by the precision of the date of Pandarus's dream and his visit as May 3. It is probably private symbolism on Chaucer's part that he uses May 3 frequently in his poetry, and it is always a day of catastrophe. In the *Nun's Priest's Tale*, the rooster-hero is seized by a fox on "May's day the third," reenacting Adam's fall in the Garden of Eden, which in some folklore took place on May 3. The same date is used in the *Knight's Tale* as the day of the perception of the object of fatal desire. The allusion to the story of Europa reinforces another aspect of the poem—its theme of origins in violence. Kidnapped and raped by Zeus (disguised as a white bull), Europa disappears, and her father sends her brother, Cadmus, to find her. In his search, Cadmus is instructed to follow a cow with a white spot and to found a city where the cow lies down. That city is Thebes, and with its foundation begins the chain of cities founded in and eventually destroyed by the violence of disordered passion. Troy is its heir.

Just as dire is the description of Pandarus, betwixt sleep and waking, dreaming one of the most savage myths, the story of Philomel, Procne, and Tereus. Raped by her brother-in-law who has also cut out her tongue, Philomel reveals the crime to her sister Procne by weaving the story into a cloth. Procne avenges her sister and herself by killing the child she has had with Tereus, cooking him in a stew, and serving the meal to her husband. In addition to incest and sexual violence, the themes of the story include betrayal of kin, the turning of brother-in-law against sister-in-law, wife against husband, mother against child. It is in this setting, metaphorically constructed, that Pandarus sets out to destroy his niece's newly won security and deliver her to the desires of his friend.

As Pandarus arrives at his niece's parlor, Chaucer once again employs classical allusion to great effect. Criseyde is found listening—somewhat anachronistically—to a reading of the *Thebiad*, a book by Statius and the Middle Ages' authoritative account of the story of Thebes. Pandarus, who reveals that he, too, has read the book, insists that Criseyde "put it away" (*TC* 111) because, we suspect, he fears it contains something unhelpful to his objective. The story of Thebes is the history of Troy's own past, and thus Criseyde's history as well. Had she read beyond the story of Oedipus, which is what she is reading when Pandarus interrupts her, she would have learned much about betrayal, deception, and failed love, and would even have met Tydeus, one of the Seven Against Thebes and father of Diomede, the man, lurking in Criseyde's future who will be her final undoing.

Although Criseyde has found security in the virtue that Hector urged upon her, she is weak in resolve and obsessively concerned with how she is regarded by others. Pandarus assails Criseyde with a barrage of sophistical stratagems geared to deceive a woman of little intelligence,

> Then he thought: "If I make my pitch too strong,
> Or too complex, or too rhetorical,
> It will not please and it may alarm her.
> She will suspect that I am deceptive,
> For the tender witted regard all that
> Is not literal as some kind of trick.
> So I will gauge my words to her weak wit." (*TC* II, 267–72)

Whatever her shortcomings, Criseyde is far from unintelligent. Daughter of a Seer, niece of a Sophist, she is every bit as shrewd and subtle as her father and uncle. The entire first scene of Book II is one in which niece and uncle try to outwit one another, he to beguile her into his plot, she to find out what he is up to without appearing curious. That Criseyde has seen through Pandarus's rhetoric and stratagems from the beginning is clear in her outburst when she finally discovers the specifics of his scheme:

> What! Is this the joyous surprise for me?
> Is this your advice, and is this my bliss?
> Is this the reward your words betoken?
> Has all your sophistry now been spoken? (*TC* II, 421–24)

Criseyde clearly perceives that her uncle is up to no good, that his concerns are not for her best interests, and that the end of his scheme is ignominious.[2]

But she goes along with it anyway!

Chaucer explains why Criseyde allows herself to be betrayed in this way: "So, Criseyde, who almost died of fright, / For, indeed, she was the fearfullest / Woman who had ever lived" (*TC* II, 449–51). Her lack of fortitude makes Criseyde a victim of the vicissitudes of this world: the politics of Troy, the opinion of her neighbors, the desires of suitors. She takes on the character of what Boethius's Lady Philosophy describes as persons tossed upon the wheel of fortune because they have failed to develop the inner life.

Like others without a sense of self, Criseyde resorts to craft and dissimulation to protect her self-interests. She is a pragmatist, a materialist, and something of a Nominalist herself. She recovers quickly from her outrage at Pandarus's scheme and begins to connive, musing on the age-old relativist's rationalization:

> The lesser of two evils best it is
> To choose. (*TC* II, 470–71)

---

[2] Shakespeare seems to have noticed this in Chaucer's depiction and developed it in his own fashioning of Cressida, where she matches her uncle's rhetorical subtleties with sophisticated repartee. See *Troilus and Cressida*, Act I, Scene 2.

Words are of great importance to Criseyde. The first thing she asks Pandarus about her would-be lover is whether Troilus "can speak well about love." Her inner deliberations as to whether to take Troilus as her lover are entirely pragmatic and selfish:

> Well I understand he is my king's son,
> And since his desire for me is so strong,
> If I refuse him, his anger I may
> Provoke and then I may well pay a price.
> A worse plight then, for sure, would I be in.
> Would it be wise, I ask, to purchase hate
> When I have the chance myself to advance? (*TC* II, 708–14)

Our Narrator becomes alarmed at the apparent crassness exhibited by the heroine and attempts to assure us that she was really far more delicate in her thoughts than he has reported. He tells us that although many might find that she gave in too easily, he believes that Criseyde only "inclined" toward Troilus and that what won her heart was really his "manhood" and the suffering he felt for her.

Because words create reality, Pandarus urges Troilus to put into words his desires in a letter to Criseyde, and teaches him many of the fine points of epistolary rhetoric. Finding numerous metaphors for Criseyde herself and a stock of hyperboles for his own feelings, Troilus bathes the letter with his tears, and, so real are words, he speaks to the letter and kisses it a thousand times: "Letter, a blissful fate for thee is shaped. / My lady shall upon thee look" (*TC* II, 1091–92).

Pandarus delivers the missile by thrusting it down Criseyde's bosom, a gesture that emphasizes the eroticism of the written words stained with Troilus's bodily tears. That words constitute the reality of passion is seen again when Criseyde finally agrees to write a letter in response. Pandarus carries these letters from one to the other, back and forth, as a prelude to the physical consummation that, in his role of go-between, he will next construct. Thus by the end of

Book Two, Pandarus has achieved one of his two goals: He has wrested control of the narrative from the Narrator who now is reduced to simply describing what his competitor creates. Pandarus's second goal, the seduction of Criseyde, awaits Book Three.

3 Troilus and Criseyde

BOOK THREE

BOOK THREE, as the structural midpoint of the five-book poem is also the narrative midpoint in which the passion of Troilus and Criseyde is consummated. It is, therefore, appropriate that Venus is invoked and that she is described both as an erotic force and as the cosmic force that creates the order of the universe. In the Middle Ages, many symbols had both a positive and a negative signification, like two sides of a coin. Venus for example was seen as *Venus Creatrix* and *Venus Fornitrix*, representing alternately the goodness of ordered eros and the disasters caused by disordered eros. In Book Three Troilus and Criseyde begin their disordered love, a disorder reflected in the very predicament of Troy brought about through another paradigmatic disordered passion, that of Paris for Helen. Subsequent books will show the disorder spreading through the lovers' lives and leading to their separate downfalls, again paralleling the fall of Troy itself initiated by the individual lawlessness of Paris and Helen.

At this point the structure of the poem seems to reveal itself as a dynamic between similitude and dissimilitude, or, as Pandarus has stated earlier, through contrariety. As the paradigm of the story of Troilus and Criseyde is that of Paris and Helen, so the anti-paradigm, or contrary, is the story of Dante and Beatrice. As the narrative progresses, the analogy to the *Commedia* becomes increasingly insistent.

At the end of the Prohemium of the third book, the Narrator seems to get confused and suddenly addresses Calliope, asking for her help to tell the joy of Troilus in Venus's service. This is another odd invocation, since Calliope is the muse of epic poetry, and not likely to be much help in rhyming romance.[1] Nor is there anything epic-like or heroic in the machinations of the pimping Pandarus as he stage-manages the consummation scene, a scene in which Venus clearly abandons the bedroom and that degenerates into burlesque. Having gained Criseyde's acquiescence to his plan, Pandarus realizes that it is time to warn the naïve Troilus to what is happening and about to happen. He does this, we see, not out of concern for his young friend, but to protect himself:

> And so for you, my boy, have I become—
> Well, somewhat to help you, somewhat for fun—
> Someone who brings women to men, a pimp,
> You know what I mean. I have lured
> My blameless niece, Criseyde, into a tryst
> So that you might have what you so desire. (*TC* III, 253–59)

Pandarus, we see, is keenly aware of the moral implications of his actions:

> And were it known that I schemed in this way,
> To have her do all such as you desire,
> Why, all the world would blame and revile me,
> And they would call me the worst of traitors.
> (*TC* III, 274–77)

---

[1] Errors of this kind by the Narrator seem to add irony to his supposed respect for sources. Calliope is invoked by Dante in the opening of *Purgatorio*, whereas, of course, in Book Three Troilus is entering the "heaven" prepared by Pandarus. In the Prohemium to Book Two, which begins with the first lines of the *Purgatorio* that precede an invocation to Calliope, our Narrator confusedly invokes Clio instead.

As he makes clear, what concerns Pandarus is not the objective harm he will cause both to his niece and to his friend, but rather the *name* that might be given to it. He does not shrink from betrayal, but he fears the word "traitor." He fully intends to procure his niece to satisfy Troilus's lust, but he cringes at the name "pimp." What is essential to maintaining Pandarus's ethical construct is the collusion of the other in agreeing that things are whatever you call them, and, in particular, that vice is really virtue by another name.

> Before I go another step in this,
> You must, upon your very life, swear that hence
> Secrecy will be our sacred motto:
> What I mean is, that you will never tell
> The truth. (*TC* III, 281–84)

Troilus proves to be a conscientious student and, sensing the promise of erotic satisfaction, quickly adopts his master's philosophy and his language along with it:

> Good grief! I hope you don't think that I would
> Call what you are up to for me pimping!
> Though I may be dumb, I am not crazy!
> Pimping! It is not so, I am convinced.
> Someone who does the same thing for money,
> Let us use the word pimp for what he does.
> Let us call what you do by other names,
> Virtue, friendship, and generosity.
> Lets make some distinctions here! We all know
> That subtle differences may be found
> Between things that appear to be the same. (*TC* III, 395–406)

Troilus's innocence perishes in this scene in which, having at last learned something of the art of sophistry from his expert teacher, he adopts the Nominalist position that virtues and vices—loyalty, honesty, betrayal, deceit—are mere abstractions assigned a name, and what one man might call a vice another might call virtue. To prove to Pandarus that his morality is as relativistic as his philosophy is Nominalist, Troilus declares his solidarity in vice by offering to pimp for him in turn:

> And, so just to prove to you that I think
> Your service no shame, no, nor any vice,
> My own sister, Polyxena the fair,
> Cassandra, Helen, or any other,
> No matter how shapely or sweet they be,
> Tell me which you want, and you shall have her.
> Let it be! (*TC* III, 407–13)

For the Middle Ages, Troilus's sisters, Polyxena and Cassandra, were noble, even holy women, both destined for heroic, self-sacrificing, tragic ends. The idea of prostituting them would have been deeply shocking to a mediaeval audience aware of the virtues of which these women were paragons. Polyxena, who, according to various legends, not only contributed her gold bracelets to ransom Hector's dead body, but offered herself as a slave to Achilles for the same purpose, was considered a model of sibling fidelity and self-sacrifice. Cassandra's integrity consisted in refusing the sexual advances of Apollo, a god, even though he had given her the gift of prophesy. Although Troilus has little concern for her virtue, even the gods were outraged when, clinging to the statue of Athena, Cassandra was raped by Ajax.

While Troilus and Pandarus are agreeing to call things by whatever name makes them seem less distasteful, Criseyde, for her part, is also accepting words in place of truth. In a familiar psychological process, Criseyde, who has all along seemed much more interested in Hector, convinces herself of Troilus's virtue and invents feelings of love for him. The Narrator explicitly states that it is Troilus's acts *and words* that Criseyde falls in love with (*TC* III, 471).

The Narrator, however, seems not to perceive the full meaning of his words nor even to remember his earlier ones. In describing the early events of Book Three, he defends the fact that he does not describe more of the emotions of Troilus on the grounds that his "author," presumably the fictitious Lollius, does not provide these details. The audience recalls, however, that in Book One the Narrator claimed to give us more of the "Canticus Troili" than he found in his source.

In order to bring the couple together physically, Pandarus invites Criseyde to his house for dinner where Troilus will be hidden. Apparently suspicious of his intentions, Criseyde asks her uncle whether Troilus will be there, and he replies that Troilus is "out of town." The Narrator comments:

> My author does not reveal all
> That she thought when he declared this,
> That Troilus had gone out of town,
> Whether this was true or a lie. (*TC* III, 575–78)

The absurdity of being "out of town" when the town is surrounded by the Greek hosts seems not to strike the Narrator, but it clearly occurs to Criseyde. Such a device accomplishes a number of things; it characterizes the Narrator once more as unreliable—either because of his stupidity or his desire to put Criseyde in a good light—and it characterizes Criseyde as an accomplice in her own seduction, since she accepts the invitation knowing full well that Troilus cannot be "out of town." Thus it is an example of a character, in this case the Narrator, "saying more than he intends," for by questioning whether Criseyde believed Pandarus's absurd lie, he shows the audience a trait in the heroine that he would have preferred to hide.

Chaucer uses this device to undermine the whole consummation scene that begins with Troilus watching Criseyde's arrival at Pandarus's house through a little window in a room Chaucer calls a "stewe." Attention has been called to the unusualness of this Middle English word used to designate, as one assumes it is meant to, a closet or small room.[2] The word comes from the Italian "stufa" and the French "étuve" meaning heater or stove and as "stewe" came to be the Middle English word for a steam-heated bathhouse. Its negative echo in this passage, in which Troilus anxiously awaits the consummation of his lust, is that "stewes" in Chaucer's time were generally brothels.

Sneaking into the room where Criseyde is sleeping, Pandarus reveals that Troilus is in the house, and that he got there "by the gutter," an infelicitous choices of word through which the Narrator unwittingly deflates the romantic setting of the couples' first embrace. The description of the actual consummation, a description the Narrator lingers over, is an even greater let down, quickly degenerating into vaudeville.

By Criseyde's bedside, Pandarus begins to prepare her for Troilus's appearance by telling still another lie, that Troilus is grieving over a rumor he has heard, that Criseyde has given her love to another. Like the Narrator, Criseyde, too, is prone to express more than she intends or understands. Upset by the lie, she pronounces a long soliloquy taken directly from Boethius (*TC* III, 813–33). The wisdom of the Boethian passage reveals the emptiness of worldly pleasures and goes on to say that those who do not realize this are ignorant, and ignorance cannot be called happiness; those who do recognize the mutability of worldly joy can rationally no longer be committed to it. With heavy irony, Chaucer has Criseyde move from this perception of a Boethian truth to a most un-Boethian entry into the joys of this world.

In a scene anticipating *opera buffa*, Pandarus enters Criseyde's bedroom through a trapdoor leading from a tunnel that connects his room with hers. Having convinced Criseyde that she must denounce the rumor of her infidelity and console Troilus personally, Pandarus has Troilus pop up from under the trapdoor where he has been hidden, and the youth falls on his knees beside

---

[2] See note to this line (III, 601) in Larry Benson, ed., *The Riverside Chaucer*, 1039.

Criseyde's bed.³ Pandarus, ever the stage manager, runs for a cushion for the kneeling lover, declaring as he goes, "We will *all* be merry soon!" (*TC* III, 952, my emphasis).

At this crucial moment, the Narrator once again interrupts the description to inform the audience that he does not know what Criseyde could have been thinking, but that, in any case, she invited Troilus to rise and sit on her bed. Pandarus, still stage-managing events, congratulates his niece for taking Troilus to her bed, since now they will be able to *hear* each other better! Making sure everything goes as planned, Pandarus sticks close to the arena of erotic action:

> So he moved aside to the fireplace
> With a candle and there pretended that
> He was reading a book, an old romance. (*TC* III, 978–80)

If Pandarus is only "pretending" to read his book, where are his eyes? Chaucer uses the scene, not only to further reveal Pandarus's voyeurism, but also to create a sophisticated intertextual allusion. Specifying Pandarus's text as an "old romance" suggests a venerable mediaeval literary tradition and universalizes the moral dimension of the lovers' passion. What, then, could it be, the "old romance" that Pandarus pretends to read?

Once the audience frames this question, a whole series of famous romances suggests itself: the *Roman de la Rose,* which Chaucer translated, the romance of *Tristam et Iseult,* and the most famous of them all, the story of Lancelot and Guinevere in Chretien de Troye's *Le Chevalier de la Charette.* Thinking of this last text leads the audience to further intertextual associations, to a couple made famous by their reading together *Le Chevalier de la Charette,* found in Dante's *Commedia.* Paolo and Francesca were

---

³ Some believe that the trapdoor is another of Pandarus's fictions, but it is difficult to see the reason for it, and in line 741 it is the Narrator, not Pandarus, who says, "Pandarus did undo a *trappe*" (trapdoor).

led into fornication by the mimetic power of the description of Lancelot and Guinevere's adultery.[4]

Chaucer has created a brilliant metaphor of reading that acts like a series of mirrors in which Pandarus, holding the written text, "reads" the erotic text of Troilus and Criseyde's fornication, a text he himself has authored, which enacts the same "old story" of Lancelot and Guinevere, Tristam and Iseult, Paolo and Francesca, and all the other illicit lovers of mediaeval literary fame.

After a long speech meant to untangle Pandarus's lie about her infidelity, Criseyde sheds "a few, bright, new-made tears" (*TC* III, 1051) and lays back in bed. Troilus understands the situation, but he is squeamish:

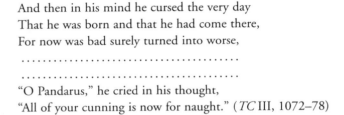

> And then in his mind he cursed the very day
> That he was born and that he had come there,
> For now was bad surely turned into worse,
> ....
> ....
> "O Pandarus," he cried in his thought,
> "All of your cunning is now for naught." (*TC* III, 1072–78)

The tearful, romantic scene turns comical when, at the moment when he should consummate his passion, our hero faints!

Pitifully and ridiculously, Pandarus attempts to save what is left of the calamitous scenario: He rushes to quiet the astonished Criseyde and, shouting, "Oh, wretch, is this a manly pose?" strips Troilus to his undershirt and throws him into bed!

The brave efforts of the Narrator to construct an epic with the help of the Muses—however confusedly invoked—and Pandarus's competing efforts to construct a Romance with the help of sophistry, have come to naught, and the whole has degenerated from these noble genres to foolish burlesque and even low farce. No epic hero this, who faints at the sight of a woman; no roman-

---

4 Dante, *Inferno* V.

tic hero, either, who cannot even get his clothes off! No remote Courtly Lady this, who must take over the erotic initiative and revive her lover from a swoon (*TC* III, 1114, 1126f).

Pandarus, too, is undermined through the burlesque collapse of his mise-en-scène. Try as he might, Pandarus never quite recovers his control over the narrative, and, from this point on, the narrative direction slides increasingly out from under Pandarus's authorial intention.

Here, at the center of the center of the text, is revealed the fullness of Chaucer's scheme. Troilus is an anti-Dante in a pilgrimage away from transcendence and toward degradation. As Dante was led by his virtuous guide out of the Wood of Error and away from a life of sensual dissipation, Troilus is led into error and self-indulgence by an anti-guide and anti-friend, a perverse Virgil motivated by prurient desire. Dante has Virgil represent the highest achievement of human intellect unaided by divine grace; Chaucer has Pandarus satirically represent the nadir to which philosophy has been brought by Nominalism. Our anti-Pilgrim moves in a contrary direction toward an anti-Beatrice who, instead of conducting him to Heaven, will drag him to a paradise of the flesh and unto death.

Not content with this brilliant inversion, Chaucer invokes other analogies and piles paradigm upon paradigm. The widespread use in the poem of lines from Boethius allows him to suggest Troilus as an anti-Boethius to whom appears, in his prison of desire, an anti-Lady Philosophy who teaches him, not how to get off the Wheel of Fortune, but how to get on.

At the same time that he employs contrariety, Chaucer suggests the complimentary similitudes: Troilus is a moral Paris making choices determined by lust; he is a new Paolo, and Criseyde a new Francesca; they are Lancelot and Guinevere; and ultimately—only generally—Adam and Eve reenacting the choice that reflects the tragedy of the human condition. Such is the allegorical reading of the poem, but that is not all the poem is. Chaucer eschews the restrictions of a single genre by employing many and by constantly undermining the very genres he introduces. Thus, if we see Troilus as a mediaeval Adam, Criseyde as Eve, Pandarus as serpent, they so ludicrously represent those figures that we cannot seriously pursue that interpretation and must turn to some other. Through this self-undermining, Chaucer leads us through a series of perceptions into the poem that, while each is inadequate, cumulatively reveal the over-arching structure.

4 Troilus and Criseyde

BOOK FOUR

BOOK FOUR RECOUNTS the descent of Troilus on Fortune's wheel ending in his loss of Criseyde. The three main characters are seen in increasingly negative light as the personage of Calkas reappears initiating the crisis of the plot, his successful demand that his daughter be sent to him in the Greek camp through a prisoner exchange.

Troilus and Pandarus are both present in the Trojan parliament when the question of whether to exchange Criseyde for the Trojan prisoner Antenor is debated, but neither speaks out to oppose the exchange. The Narrator tells us that Troilus is struck dumb by shame: He is silent, "lest men should suspect his passion" (*TC* IV, 153–54). Things that are done in secret may not bear the light of public revelation. Added to this, we are told, Troilus was impotent because "He didn't have Criseyde's permission to speak!" (*TC* IV, 165). Hector, however, doesn't need a woman's permission to speak in public and feels no such scruples because his intentions are honorable: "Tell the Greeks we Trojans don't sell women!" (*TC* IV, 181).

He is, as we know, sadly mistaken, for the Trojans do, indeed, trade in women, beginning with Helen and including Criseyde, and it is determined that she will go to the Greeks. Chaucer makes sure that the audience does not miss the irony that

Criseyde, who will betray Troilus in the Greek camp, is swapped for the arch-traitor, Antenor, who will betray Troy and make possible its destruction by the Greeks.[1]

In face of this crisis, our hero once again takes to his bed where, as in Book One, Pandarus finds him whimpering and blaming Fortune for his loss. Still deforming Boethian ideas, Pandarus invokes the theory of the commonality of Fortune that Lady Philosophy uses to teach the grieving Boethius that since all worldly goods are Fortune's gifts and belong to no man in his own right, it is unreasonable to bemoan their loss. This is meant as a further lesson on the insubstantiality of worldly delights. Pandarus's version drives the lesson in the opposite direction and encourages cynical hedonism:

> What have you got to complain about now?
> Why do you snivel and whimper this way?
> You got what you wanted, so now move on! (*TC* IV, 393–95)

True to his relativist worldview, Pandarus tries to console Troilus with the idea that one woman is as good as another—the equivalent of the modern cliché, "They're a dime a dozen," and he, the Pandar, will be glad to get Troilus another:

> You know, I'm sure, that this fair town is full
> Of ladies of all kinds who, in my view,
> Are more sweet than twelve of her whom you've lost.
> I'll get you one – don't fret—or even two. (*TC* IV, 400–403)

---

1 Antenor plotted to remove from Troy the Palladium, a sacred statue of Pallas Athena that guaranteed that as long as it remained in place, Troy could never be overcome. One wonders whether Chaucer was aware of the tradition that Antenor, disgusted by Deiphobus's rape of Helen after the death of his brother, Paris, was motivated to betray his city because of its moral degeneracy.

Pandarus's one virtue is consistency. In morality, even as in metaphysics, he is ever the Nominalist. Reality consists in the human experience of individual things to which experiences we attach names. Love is nothing more than the delight Troilus takes in Criseyde, and perhaps, Marjorie, and Alison, and Mabelle, too, and all the others whom Pandarus can, no doubt, provide.

Pandarus, however, has underestimated the depth of Troilus's obsession with Criseyde, and he fails to persuade the lover to transfer his desires to other objects. So he changes tactics and advises Troilus to "act like a man" and carry Criseyde away with him:

> That could not be called rape, nor vice at all,
> To seize the one you love and run away
> ....
> Think how brother, Paris, got his lover!
> Why should you not, like him, have another?
> (*TC* IV, 596–97; 608–9)

Pandarus is not discouraged. He does not care whether Troilus adopts one strategy or another, as long as he gets to stage-manage the project. And so, when Troilus insists that he must have Criseyde and no other, Pandarus sets about it:

> Cheer up, and let me work at this business,
> For I shall shape it that tonight somehow
> You speak with your lady and know her will. (*TC* IV, 651–53)

Pandarus has two possible scenarios in mind: he instructs Criseyde to tell Troilus either that she will find a way not to go, or that she will soon return. It does not matter which she uses, according to Pandarus, because neither is true, but one or the other with allow Pandarus to temporize.

Book Four is filled with melodrama. A central scene has Criseyde tear her hair, threaten suicide, say she will starve, dress in black, and all other kinds of theatrics, yet she vetoes every practical plan to keep her in Troy. At the height of her hysteria, she faints, and Troilus, apparently believing she is dead, begins his own theatrics:

> His sword out of its sheath at last he drew
> To kill himself, so desperate was he,
> So that his soul with hers might reunite. (*TC* IV, 1185–87)

But not before a speech! Troilus denounces Jove, Fortune, and life itself. He bids farewell to Troy, to Priam, to Hecuba, and raises his sword for the fatal blow. Regaining consciousness at just the right moment, Criseyde cries out her lover's name and thus stays his hand. At this point, melodrama turns into parody:

> She saw his sword and asked why it was drawn.
> He said he would have died if died had she,
> And she gazed on him and clasped him to her,
> . . . .
> You mean, had I not woke, you would have slain
> Yourself? For me? (*TC* IV, 1224f)

Such a scene in the work of a poet as ironic as Chaucer can only be intended to undermine itself, and whatever temptation there may be to read it seriously must be resisted. In revealing the emotions of the lovers as shallow and histrionic, Chaucer prepares us for the reversal of the scene's sentimentality.

The utter lack of true sentiment on Criseyde's part is forcefully brought out in the subsequent dialogue between the lovers in which they attempt to solve the problem of the edict. Whatever regrets Criseyde may have about leaving Troy and Troilus, they are nothing in comparison to her preoccupations over her own safety and self-interests. Criseyde's plan is to agree to go to her father in the Greek camp, but, as she tells Troilus, to return in "a week or two" (*TC* IV, 1278). Tongue in cheek, Chaucer has Criseyde assure Troilus that hers are only suggestions and that he, Troilus, is the man in charge and shall make the final decision. She then begins a detailed description of a plan to return to Troy that is transparently impossible. In her enthusiasm for convincing Troilus of her plan, Criseyde becomes the main advocate for her own banishment. In its baffling logic, Criseyde's scenario involves numerous considerations: Parliament has decided I must go, so I must; the Greek camp isn't far away; I'll write; I'll be gone only ten days; the war may soon be over, and so on.

When all of this apparently fails to convince Troilus, Criseyde constructs an even more fantastic plot in which she will outwit her father by playing on his vices. Calkas is materialistic and covetous, so she will tell him she wants to return to Troy to bring back to him the possessions he has left behind. Criseyde grows philosophical as she spins this plan and reflects on the nature of language:

> If Calkas tries oracles to test me,
> I will whine and dun and pester him,
> And convince him that he misunderstands,
> For language of gods is ambiguous,
> Half the time they lie, half they tell the truth. (*TC* IV, 1401–7)

The ambiguity of language that Criseyde attributes to the gods is equally present in the words of men, as both she and her uncle demonstrate, and it is this ambiguity that makes it possible to construe the world the way it needs to be to achieve one's desires. In the present case, Criseyde's words are intended to create enough ambiguity in Troilus's mind about the possibility of her return so as to prevent him from taking any definitive action to prevent her departure, which, she fears, would reveal the couple's illicit relation and harm her reputation. Criseyde also believes that what must be, must be. She is not only a victim of fortune and predestination, but their agent. She intends at all cost to stop her lover from taking action and thus changing the direction of events. The possibility that Troilus might become an agent in time and history rather than its victim is effectively destroyed by Criseyde's own fatalism and the clever rhetoric used to enforce it.

Like her uncle, Criseyde views reality as the simulacrum of language. Indeed, there are no gods, only names of gods. As she states,

Fear first created the gods, I suppose. (*TC* IV, 1407)

Criseyde's atheism follows from her general worldview. She is a materialist who believes that there is nothing more to reality than what human physical experience reveals. She has learned to manipulate the situations she finds herself in to her advantage, since virtue, love, honor, integrity are mere words that when relied upon prove to bring about nothing advantageous. What is real for Criseyde is what is outside of herself, not the inner self, and this is the source of her insecurity, the cause the makes her "the fearfullest creature who ever lived." Moreover, in using this saying, "fear first created the gods," Criseyde is echoing Capaneus, one of the seven against Thebes, famous for his hatred of the gods. While the saying is found in several sources, we know that Chaucer's primary source for the story of Thebes was Statius's *Thebiad*, and there we hear Capaneus, lusting for war, denounce the warnings of auguries against it, with the phrase, "primus in orbe deos fecit timor" (fear first made gods in the world) (*Thebiad* III, 621).

We know, of course, from the exchange between Pandarus and his niece in Book Two that Criseyde is familiar with Statius because her uncle interrupts her reading of the *Thebiad*. We also know from details of what she has just read that she has finished book seven of Statius's account. Therefore she has read the lines from book three in which the "young blasphemer" (*Thebiad* III, 621) proclaims the gods a fiction, and we realize that Criseyde is quoting Capaneus. Because she allowed Pandarus to distract her from her reading, she could not have known that in book ten, he whom she quotes defies Jupiter and is struck dead by the god's thunderbolt.[2] Dante has

---

2 Statius, *Thebiad*, ed. and trans D. R. Shackleton Bailey, 2 vols. (Cambridge, MA: Harvard University Press/Loeb Classical Library, 2003), Book 10, 904–28.

Capaneus in the seventh circle of Hell for the sin of having done violence to the gods.

Troilus's reaction to Criseyde's plan shows that, feckless as he is, Troilus is not totally besotted. He understands perfectly that his lover's scheme is impossible, and says so, but such is the numbing power of desire that we come to believe what we know is untrue. His alternate plan is simple and straightforward: Let's not risk the possibility that you will not be able to return, let's steal away together.

This is, of course, the safer plan since there are many things that could go awry in Criseyde's scheme to return, and therefore Troilus's logic seems sound. What he does not consider, unlike his lover, is that Criseyde's plan has fewer risks to *herself*, and that is why she prefers it.

Book Four ends with increasingly distressing examples of Criseyde's shallowness. Because, as she has proclaimed, she does not believe in the existence of the gods, Criseyde does not hesitate to swear an oath to them:

> So I swear to every god celestial,
> And to every goddess in the same way,
> . . . .
> That Atropos my thread of life cut off
> If I be false. (*TC* IV, 1541–47)

As the audience that has heard her cold calculations of the pros and cons of loving Troilus, we cringe to hear her declare the nobility of her affections:

> Be well assured, t'was not your royal estate
> Nor pleasure, nor your prowess in battle,
> Not status, not prestige, nor even money
> Made me look with mercy on your longing,
> But moral virtue, well grounded in truth—
> That alone was my consideration. (*TC* IV, 1667–72)

Chaucer has structured his romance-epic in five books reflecting the five-book structure of Boethius's *Consolation of Philosophy*. This imitation is confirmed by the content of the poem in which Troilus's fortunes rise from a low point in Book One to their zenith in Book Three and to their disastrous depths in Book Five. This narrative motion reflects the turning of the Wheel of Fortune, Boethius's central metaphor. Moreover, Chaucer has so crafted the poem that, along with the rise and fall of the hero, we see the parallel revolution of the Narrator who, undermined by Chaucer-Author, loses control of the plot to Pandarus in Book Two and, as we will see, seizes it back briefly in Book Five. Thus the "fortunes" of the Narrator advance in the opposite direction to those of the hero—down and up; rather than up, then down. But, further, we see that Pandarus's progress follows a trajectory similar to Troilus's. His ascendancy toward control of the narrative begins in Book Two, is complete in Book Three, declines in Book Four, and collapses in Book Five. Thus, although the structural dynamic of *Troilus and Criseyde* mirrors that of the *Consolation of Philosophy*, the moral trajectory of the characters is the opposite. Boethius moves from the high point of worldly fame and prosperity to the low point of unjust destitution and finally up to true happiness through the transcendence of mutability. Troilus moves up from the "bad fortune" of unrequited love to the "good fortune" of erotic consummation and finally down to the loss of both love and life.

5 Troilus and Criseyde

BOOK FIVE

THE NARRATIVE of the last book opens at dawn on the day that Criseyde is to be exchanged for Antenor, and we meet the fascinating and important secondary character Diomede, whose task it will be to lead Criseyde into the Greek camp. Intensifying the drama of the scene is the fact that Troilus is chosen to lead Criseyde out of Troy and to deliver her into the hands of his Greek enemy.

Chaucer achieves a powerful tableau in describing the moment when Diomede reaches out and seizes the reins of Criseyde's horse. Pleading once more with Criseyde not to betray him, Troilus,

> With that, pale of face, his steed he turned 'round,
> And without a word to Diomede, fled;
> Of which the son of Tydeus took note,
> For he was perceptive and understood
> More than meets the eye where guile is present;
> So this Diomede seized her by the reins. (*TC* V, 85–90)

Diomede, whose name means *god-like cunning*, is presented in legend as a wiley character, possessed both of strength of body and power of words. Chaucer calls him "large of tongue," suggesting, perhaps, that he is a "smooth talker." His persona cries out virility, all the more striking, perhaps, since there is so little of it apparent in the other characters in the poem. But his virility is merely physical, and tradition portrays him as libidinous and crafty. In a remarkable interior monologue, Chaucer considerably expands Diomede's character:

> Diomede, who led her by the bridel,
> When he saw the Trojans all ride away,
> Thought to himself, "it is no waste of time
> To try my hand somewhat with a few words.
> It will at least help pass the time away,
> For over and over I have heard said,
> Nothing ventured, nothing gained." (*TC* V, 92–98)

The image of seizing the reins and leading Criseyde by the bridle bespeaks control and domination and prefigures the mastery that Diomede seeks and will soon gain over her.

Once again, Chaucer delineates a character in intriguing psychological terms. Diomede's attraction to Criseyde, we learn, has all to do with what he has gleaned from the behavior of Troilus in the moment of exchange.

> He sensed what was afoot and he thought thus,
> "I will let the cat out of the bag
> If I speak of love or make my pitch too strong.
> For if she has at heart him whom I think,
> I may not be able to rout him fast.
> So I will gauge my words in such a way
> That she will not yet catch on to my scheme." (*TC* V, 99–105)

Later on, still conniving at his seduction, Diomede mentally plots his strategy;

> This Diomede, whom I described before,
> Within himself began to cogitate
> With all the sophistry he could muster,
> How to find the best way and the quickest
> To snare Criseyde's heart within his net.

This was his sole and constant thought, how to
Lay out hook and line and snag that little fish. (*TC* V, 771–77)

Observing her and perceiving that she is preoccupied, Diomede guesses that she has a lover in Troy, and for him, this is her chief attraction:

"Whoso might snatch away such a flower
From him for whom she languishes all day
Might well boast and call himself the victor!" (*TC* V, 792–94)

In this remarkable interior monologue we see the peculiar psychology of a character whose appetite is aroused by the fact that the object of desire belongs to another man. This is the psychology of what René Girard has called "mimetic desire" in which the *vaniteux* desires a thing, not for itself, but because it belongs to another whom he desires to be, but has taken as a rival. In this strange but frequent dynamic, the object of desire is not what is really desired, but is a means to the real object of desire: the rival.[1]

There is obviously a strong vicarious element in such a mentality, and this is reinforced by the calculations of Diomede, which echo exactly the thoughts of Pandarus as he began the verbal seduction of Criseyde in Book Two. Both men assume that their subtlety is greater than hers, and that through deceitful rhetoric and lying words, they can beguile her to their own ends. But the similarity between Pandarus and Diomede does not end there; each man's pleasure draws its breath from the erotic life of Troilus, and in that their pleasure is vicarious. The dissimilitude between the two is equally strong: Diomede is *testif,* virtually pulsating with sexual force, whereas Pandarus's strength is all blabber and words that have no potency, signifying nothing.

---

[1] René Girard, *Deceit, Desire, and the Novel* (Baltimore: Johns Hopkins University Press, 1966). English translation of *Mensonge romantique, verité Romanesque* (Paris: Grasset, 1961).

Diomede's assault upon Criseyde is strategically effective. Perceiving her isolation, he offers her "friendship" (*TC* V, 128); sensing her insecurity, he will be like a "brother" (*TC* V, 134); and, appealing to her sentiments, he will be her "servant" (*TC* V, 146, 173). Bringing his wooing to a close, Diomede makes a declaration with which, we suppose, Chaucer intended to astonish the audience:

> Give me your hand; I will yours always be,
> Yours alone, no other woman for me.
> Never have I said thus to another! (*TC* V, 152–55)

Diomede's bold lie brings once again the entire historico-mythic background of the poem to the foreground, for many in Chaucer's audience will recall that Diomede was one of the original suitors of Helen. Through this device Chaucer brings Helen onstage again, as it were, in the audience's mind, making her parallel to Criseyde through the connection to Diomede.

It is also significant that Diomede, "of tongue large," metaphorizes language in a way that reveals its sophistical possibilities when he refers to Calkas's prophesy:

> "Unless Calkas tricks us with ambages,
> That is, sly words with a double meaning,
> Words that we have all learned to call 'two faced.'" (*TC* V, 897–99)

Words are two-faced when used by speakers who are two-faced, when their ambiguity is manipulated in such a way as to lead the listener to a misunderstanding. This is, as we have seen, the way that Pandarus uses words, but it is also the way that Diomede uses them, both with the intention of misleading Criseyde into the error of believing that they have her interests at heart.

In sharp contrast to Diomede's bold initiative, Troilus is found back in Troy in his chamber where, once again, he goes to bed, where he weeps and twists and turns. A discouraged Narrator, fatigued perhaps, from his long struggle with Pandarus, throws up

his hands and admits that he is unable to describe the depth of
Troilus's woe, and turns the task over to the audience:

> Who can tell fully or fully describe
> The pain of Troilus, his grief and his gall?
> Not all the men who live or ever lived!
> So to you, reader, I must leave the task
> To imagine what I cannot describe. (*TC* V, 267–71)

In a loud echo of Book One, Pandarus comes upon the sobbing
Troilus and quickly sets about creating a new reality in which
desire and gratification follow one another in an automatic way.

Troilus has had prophetic dreams that have convinced him that
Criseyde will never return, and so he asks Pandarus to prepare his
funeral. The mediaeval debate on the significance of dreams is
one that intrigued Chaucer and that he used frequently in his
writing. The traditional view, adopted by most poets, was estab-
lished in the classical period and handed down to the Middle
Ages by Macrobius, a fifth-century philosopher who wrote a commentary on Cicero's *Dream of Scipio* in which he created a set of
categories of the different types of dreams. Among those categories were types of dreams with no further significance than
indigestion from the evening meal; but there were also types of
dreams that brought information from the other world, and still
others that revealed the objective truth about happenings in the
mundane world.

In Chaucer's time, the empirical view of dreams rejected all but
those of somatic origin, a view Chaucer represents and satirizes by
putting it in the beak of a garrulous hen, as we will see when we
look at the *Canterbury Tales*. Such a view has behind it the nominalistic idea that what is real is what is, or can be, experienced by
human beings in this world of individual things. The signs and
figures in a dream, therefore, can only correspond to material,
physical causes experienced by the dreamer. Thus, for the skeptic,
all dreams are what Macrobius's described as the lowest type of

dream, the *insomnium*, or nightmare, caused by an imbalance of bodily humors. But for Macrobius himself, and for all those who believed in something beyond the physical world, several other kinds of dreams existed, including the *somnium*, which revealed, through the interpretation of the enigmatic signs within it, the meaning of events in this world.

Naturally, Pandarus adopts the skeptical view of Troilus's dreams because he wants no interference of objective reality as he tries to construct still another subjective reality in which he can retain Troilus as his marionette:

> And as for your dreams and all such nonsense,
> Drive them from your mind! Fie on them, I say!
> For they are caused by your melancholy
> Which perturbs you while you are asleep.
> There is no meaning in any kind of dream,
> Nor any man who can interpret them. (*TC* V, 358–63)

Pandarus enumerates the various theories concerning dreams— the theory of religious meaning, the scientific analysis, the idea that they are caused by the planets and the stars. As we have learned to expect from him, Pandarus concludes that given the sheer number of theories concerning dreams, Troilus should adopt a relativistic, skeptical attitude. Finally Pandarus associates all dreams with

> Old wives,
> And their beliefs in auguries of birds,
> For fear of which they think they soon shall die,
> From cries of ravens and the screech of owls,
> Ah! That a creature as noble as man
> Should believe such ordure is a disgrace! (*TC* V, 379–85)

It is not that Pandarus believes that dreams are without relation to truth; rather, he does not believe there is truth. Pandarus wants Troilus to believe what will help him advance his plot and continue his control. Troilus recounts a particularly vivid dream in which he sees Criseyde lying with a wild boar and kissing him. Troilus takes the dream as a revelation that Criseyde has betrayed him, but Pandarus asserts an alternate interpretation, and suggests that, since there can be more than one interpretation of the text of a dream, there can be no one true meaning. But a far more skillful and more honest oneiromancer is at hand:

> Cassandra smiled and said "Oh brother dear,
> If you really desire to know the truth,
> You will have to hear a few old stories,
> To wit, how that Fortune has overthrown
> So many ancient lords, and from that tale
> You will well understand who that boar is,
> For that is all written in a book." (*TC* V, 1457–63)

The book in question is, once again, Statius's *Thebiad*, the same one Pandarus prevented Criseyde from reading in Book One. Cassandra goes on to recount much of the mythology of the House of Calydon and how its emblem became the wild boar. She tells Troilus the story of the Seven Against Thebes in which, to unseat Eteocles, son of Oedipus, from the throne of Thebes, seven of the world's great champions attacked the city, and how one of the casualties, Tydeus, King of Calydon and Argos, left behind a son and heir, Diomede, to bear the emblem of the royal house. Unlike Pandarus's exegesis, Cassandra's method of interpretation relies upon history, tradition, and symbolic analysis. In this way she correctly interprets Troilus's dream:

> This very boar betokens Diomede,
> Tydeus' son, heir of Meleagre,
> He who slew the Caladonian boar.
> Diomede has your lady's affections,
> Whether you like it, or whether you don't,
> This Diomede is in and you are out! (*TC* V, 1513–18)

Against this, Pandarus counsels Troilus to believe what neither Pandarus himself believes, nor Troilus, nor the audience—that Criseyde will return in ten days as promised. And meanwhile, Pandarus will erect his next spectacle, which will have as its setting Sarpedoun's house of pleasure in which wine, women, and song are in abundance (*TC* V, 435–46).

This ancient "brothel solution" to a young man's love sickness fails in this case, for Troilus continues to long for his lost love. After four days at Sarpedoun's "feste," Troilus pleads to go home, and a week later Pandarus permits their return.

Troilus consoles himself with simulacra; he rereads old letters, recalls Criseyde's feminine charms, her "shape," and every word they had exchanged. Even Criseyde's former house becomes her proxy, and Troilus addresses its architectural details as if they were parts of Criseyde's body, ending with a wish to be able to embrace and kiss the doors of the house.[2]

The Narrator, who has so often insisted on his reliance on his "sources" and has denied originality in his retelling, now, at the moment of Criseyde's betrayal of Troilus, finds the truth of those sources unbearable. All of the sources of the story clearly blame Criseyde, not only for betraying her lover, but for breaking her oath to the gods that she would not do so. Benoit de Saint-Maure declares "she did great evil";[3] Boccaccio calls her "base Criseida, a worthless woman."[4] Desire to protect Criseyde from such judgments leads the Narrator to reject the authority of his sources and the entire literary tradition surrounding the subject.

> I will not blame this wonderful woman
> More than the narrative already shows.
> Her name, alas, is condemned, far and wide,

---

[2] This "address to the door" is, in fact, an impressive example of Chaucer's employment of "paraclausithyron," a formal figure of classical rhetoric.

[3] Benoit de Saint-Maure, *Le Roman de Troie* in *The Story of Troilus*, ed. R. K. Gordon, (New York: E. P. Dutton & Co., 1964), 19.

[4] *Il Filostrato* in ibid., 124–25.

So let this be sufficient for her crime.
Could I but find the slightest excuse—
Perhaps she regretted her betrayal—
Then I would excuse her altogether! (*TC* V, 1093–99)

We glimpse here the rather comical contradiction between the Narrator's declared objectivity and lack of feeling, and the sudden onslaught of emotions that seem to have led him to become Criseyde's self-appointed advocate and champion. He confesses that his pen "trembles as he writes," hardly the *sang-froid* of an indifferent translator.

Criseyde quickly gives in to Diomede, and as a token of her new fidelity pins upon his cloak the broach that Troilus gave her when she left Troy, a gift that was a sign of fidelity in love. The callousness of feeling that such an act reveals disgusts even our indulgent Narrator who proclaims, "That was hardly necessary!" (*TC* V, 1040). It is upon seeing this broach on his enemy that Troilus understands that Cassandra's interpretation of his dream was, indeed, true, and that Pandarus was wrong about the nature of dreams. It is here that Troilus begins to separate himself from his mentor, pointing out to him that he was wrong about the dream, wrong about Criseyde's return, wrong about the possibility of forgetting her. Pandarus's ultimate scenario has failed. He can no longer control his characters, and his newest narrative collapses. Like a balloon losing air, Pandarus actually runs out of words, and without words, he is nothing. Thus he sputters out of the narrative with a most inadequate of parting lines, "Indeed, I hate Criseyde. . . . I can say no more" (*TC* V, 1732, 1743).

Employing the device of the naïve narrator, Chaucer-Poet has been able to conceal himself throughout much of the poem. Perhaps amused by this device, Chaucer complicates it by adding another line of concealment in which Pandarus takes over the development of the narrative and pushes Chaucer-Narrator into the background. We now have a metaphoric tableau of the true

Author behind a flawed Narrator, behind a sophistical stage manager. Now that Pandarus has run out of words, the Narrator is able to reassert the little authority he once possessed. With Pandarus's decisive "I can say no more!" (*TC* V, 1743), the Narrator picks up the story line with a description of the battle between Trojans and Greeks that he soon lets lapse into still another plea to forgive Criseyde and, given the context, a rather inappropriate warning to women about the falseness of men! At this point Chaucer-Poet seems to have had enough of his bumbling Narrator and steps from behind the curtains, as it were, to conclude the book. He does so with a classic authorial "envoi" of the poem:[5]

> Go little book, go little tragedy,
> Where God may give your author, ere he die,
> The gift to put some comedy in art.
> But you, little book, must envy nothing,
> But be subject to Poetry itself,
> And kiss the steps where ascend the masters,
> Virgil, Ovid, Homer, Lucan, Statius. (*TC* V, 1786–92)

Now out in the open and beyond irony, Chaucer reveals the tradition he admires and the canon he aspires to join, and in saluting this classical pantheon, he reveals still more—his debt to other, more contemporary members of the same tradition, Boethius, Dante, Petrarch, and Boccaccio. But the Narrator is not to be got rid of so easily: "As I was saying!" (*TC* V, 1800), he protests after he has been interrupted by the Author, and picks up again the narrative of the battle in which Troilus is slain and his soul rises up through the spheres to some point from which he looks back on Earth:

> And down from there he began to gaze at
> This little spot of Earth that with the sea

---

[5] A traditional rhetorical device, the *envoi* is found in Boccaccio and reaches back at least as far as to Ovid.

Is all surrounded, and he had contempt
For this poor world where all is vanity
Compared with the joy that is in heaven.
And then as he gazed his eye hit upon
That place where he had died in battle.
And in himself he laughed at the very woe
Of those who wept in grief for his sad death. (*TC* V, 1814–22)

How could such a description not bring to the minds of Chaucer's mediaeval audience or any other literate persons the following lines?

With face turned back toward the seven spheres
I saw this little globe of earth and
I smiled at its poor semblance.
Who holds it least, is most to be admired.
(*Paradiso* XXII, 133–36)[6]

As has been the case with all of Chaucer's allusions, here the setting and words of Dante and Troilus are similar, but the sentiments are opposite. While Dante views the world from the perspective of transcendental understanding, Troilus views the world—and those who loved him—with bitter disdain. Chaucer expresses the difference through the contrast between Dante's charitable "smile" as he gazes of the earth and Troilus's sardonic "laugh."

Just as Chaucer-Poet comes out from behind Chaucer-Narrator, who has come out from behind Pandarus, so now the genuine sources of the poem—Boethius, Dante, Boccaccio, though never revealed by name—come out from behind the false—Lollius, Dares, Dictes.

The Narrator's voice is finally hushed after he has repeated the hollow sentiments from the end of *Il Filostrato* that condemn desire and the fickleness of women in particular. In contrast, the

---

[6] The echo here is complex since the flight of the soul is found in many sources that Chaucer probably knew. Chaucer's description echoes Boccaccio's (*Teseida*), which is derived from Dante (*Paradiso* XX), which itself may be derived from Lucan and others.

voice of Chaucer-Poet takes over again with the expression of deeply religious sentiments:

> Give your love to Him who for love of you,
> Did die on the cross to redeem our souls.
> He died, He rose, He now sits in heaven,
> Never unfaithful, He, to him who
> Surrenders his heart entirely to Him.
> Since it is He who is the best to love,
> What need is there to seek love's counterfeits? (*TC* V, 1842–48)

The capacity of language to mislead and to misrepresent through ignorance and deceit, represented respectively by the Narrator's incompetence and by Pandarus's sophisticated Nominalism, has now been transcended, and the Realist power of language is made evident in the concluding stanzas where love, faith, honor, and truth are expressed as objective realities possessing real existence. For a poem that has dramatized the catastrophe of the separation of word from truth, of promise from act, of signification from meaning, what better, more redemptive ending than Chaucer's word for word translation of lines from Dante's *Paradiso* (XIV, 28–30):

> Thou ever living One, and Two, and Three,
> Who reigns always as Three, and Two, and One,
> Uncircumscribed, yet all circumscribing. (*TC* V, 1863–65)

These first three lines of the closing stanza bespeak the transcendence of ambiguity in which the aporia of one being two and both being three, of something beyond limit, yet the source of all limits, are—not logically resolved—but spiritually penetrated. Chaucer completes the final stanza by combining poetry with prayer, two uses of language based on this Realist sense of words as conduits to the real rather than constructs of the real. He parallels the paradox of virginity and motherhood to God's simplicity and multiplicity, limitlessness and limit, rendering the whole as a poetic expression of the mystical definition of God as the *coincidentia oppositorum*—the coming together of all opposites and contraries. The final defeat of Pandarus's Nominalist sophistical formula, "By its contrary is everything defined," is achieved in these lines, and through this defeat language is redeemed by poetry:

> Thou ever living One, and Two, and Three,
> Who reigns always as Three, and Two, and One,
> Uncircumscribed, yet all circumscribing,
> From foes visible and invisible
> Protect us all, and for the love of Mary,
> Virgin mother, have mercy on us,
> AMEN. (*TC* V, 1863–69)

CANTERBURY TALES

6 Canterbury Tales

GENERAL PROLOGUE

ALONG WITH SEVERAL other devices that Chaucer employed in *Troilus and Criseyde*, the naïve Narrator reappears in the *Canterbury Tales* but now managed in an even more sophisticated way. In the later work Chaucer uses the structuring device of the "framed tales" in which several stories are told within the context of a larger story—the frame. In the *Canterbury Tales*, a Narrator purports to relate what happened on a pilgrimage he undertook from London to Canterbury during which he and other pilgrims told stories along the way. As in *Troilus and Criseyde*, here the Narrator is increasingly undermined and made to look foolish, but now the author goes so far as to give the Narrator a name—Geoffrey! The comic irony of a dull-witted Narrator whose name is that of the Author who controls the entire work is, of course, enormous, but beyond irony the device handled this way raises intriguing questions about the roles of author, audience, and poetic intention.

One of the central philosophical concerns of the *Canterbury Tales*, like that of *Troilus and Criseyde*, remains the nature of the relationship between reality and language, although some tales probe this theme more deeply than others. For our purposes, *The Wyf of Bath's Tale, The Pardoner's Tale,* and *The Nun's Priest's Tale* will serve to show how Chaucer develops this theme.

The work begins with an introductory section in which, as in the *Troilus*, the Narrator introduces himself, explains his intention, and the literary methods he will use to achieve it. Again, as in the earlier poem, the audience is made conspicuous by the Narrator addressing it directly and often. The General Prologue opens with the famous description of Spring in which life reawakens at every level of existence: the mineral, where rain pierces the dry ground; the vegetal, where flowers spring from the damp ground; the animal, where birds sing and mate; and, finally, the human, where mankind comes alive—not at the level of physical nature, but at the level symbolized by spiritual journey: "Then folk long to go on pilgrimages" (*Canterbury Tales* [*CT*] General Prologue [GP], 12). This image of religious devotion as natural to man, just as blooming is natural to flowers, alerts us to the general ethos of the poem, one that is captured by its governing metaphor, the pilgrimage. The movement of Chaucer's characters from London to Canterbury provides the structure of the work at the same time it symbolizes the pilgrimage of life.

Our Narrator claims to have encountered a group of pilgrims on their way to Canterbury and joined them, and says he will describe to us what he saw and heard on the journey:

> But even so, while I have time and space
> Before I further in this story pace,
> It seems the reasonable thing to do,
> To describe the whole condition to you
> Of each pilgrim, or as it seemed to me,
> And who they were, and of what degree,
> And also in what way that they were dressed (*CT* GP, 35–41)

When the Narrator refers to his own subjectivity by declaring that he will describe things not necessarily as they really were, but as they *seemed* to him, the audience has its first hint of the possibility that his account will be unreliable. Chaucer, however, undermines his Narrator in a complex and subtle way, mainly by combining his errors and faux pas with correct or meaningful declarations and judgments, although the Narrator himself is usually unaware of the rightness or wrongness of his words. For instance, when he says that he will describe the "degree" of each pilgrim, the Narrator seems to mean the social station of the character, since that is what he goes on to do. As the poem progresses, however, we see that the descriptions he provides inform us of more—the pilgrim's moral "degree" and his and her spiritual "degree," concepts common to the Middle Ages. The "naïveté" of the Narrator consists in the fact that he creates these descriptions without himself understanding all that he is revealing.

Chaucer's method of description depends heavily on physiognomy—the "reading" of the body to interpret the inner character of the person. The belief that the outer form of a thing (in this case, physical features) can express the inner psychological, spiritual truth, depends in turn on the astrological belief that the position of the planets at the moment of birth influences the psychological disposition and physical appearance of a person and that these accord with one another. Both of these ideas reflect the general understanding that everything in existence is related through an overarching harmony made possible by the fact that the One True God created everything that exists. This is another expression of the microcosm/macrocosm dynamic, similar to the Troilus/Troy image that we saw in the earlier poem, wherein the human body is seen as a "little world" reflecting the entire universe.

In astrology what accounts for the differences in temperament and behavior among individuals is the position of one planet relative to another at the moment of birth which causes a predominance of one "humor" over another in the body. The Humors—blood, yellow bile, phlegm, and black bile—are thus the correspondents to the four basic elements of the physical universe—air, fire, water, and earth—and are associated with the mythological characteristics of the planets; Mars, for instance, is associated with the color red and with blood, and the physiognomy of those whose birth he attends is likely to be ruddy of complexion and "sanguine" of temperament.

The worldview that produces the concept of physiognomy is a profoundly symbolic one in which every individual thing in the world betokens something more, beyond the world, of which it is a part. The fullness of being of the individual is found when its relation to the whole of which it is a part is made manifest.

In the General Prologue, Chaucer manipulates this device in such a way as to have his Narrator describe each character in both moral and physical terms, but in different proportions. The description of one character may be, for instance, disproportionately physical; when this character reveals himself or herself through the tale he or she tells, more often than not a sensual, physical self is revealed. Thus the descriptions of the characters in the General Prologue reveal the nature of the tellers and foreshadow their tales.

Our Narrator, who has promised to tell his story "according to reason," reasonably begins his descriptions with the representative of the highest social rank on the pilgrimage, the Knight:

> A Knight there was, and he a worthy man,
> Who from the beginning of his knighthood
> Valued truth, honor, liberality
> And courteous behavior. (*CT* GP, 43–45)

We note that what we first come to know about the Knight is his moral condition. In fact, there are in the whole portrait of thirty-six lines only four devoted to his physical appearance:

> But, so now to tell you of his array
> His horses were sound, he was not fancy.
> He wore a tunic that was of plain cloth
> Stained all over by his coat of mail. (*CT* GP, 73–76)

We are left with the impression that the essence of the man is moral and spiritual, and that he is frugal in his physical indulgences. If we compare his description to that of his son, the young Squire, we see the rhetorical strategy inverted:

> With him there was his son, a young squire,
> A young bachelor who loved the ladies.
> With a curling iron he curled his hair.
> He was about twenty years old, I think.
> Of his stature, he was of average height,
> And very agile and of great strength. (*CT* GP, 79–84)

The structure of the description here is the opposite of the first. The young man is, we understand, sensual, self-indulgent, and a bit of a dandy.

When we get to the portrait of the Wyf of Bath, we see not only the descriptive technique used for the Knight and the Squire, but a whole series of other devices used to create this unforgettable persona:

> A good-wife was there from just beside Bath.
> She was somewhat deaf, ah, what a pity!

The rhetorical awkwardness of these lines is itself a meaningful device. The effect of the Wyf being from *nearby* Bath is a detail so unnecessary to the portrait as to make us wonder whether there is some hidden importance in it. The added non sequitur that she was a bit deaf seems a random detail, that seems also to demand explanation. One would be that we are dealing with a Narrator without rhetorical skill, and at the literal level that is probably correct. But the audience also knows that behind the Narrator is the most famous and celebrated poet of his time, so something must be up! To an audience immersed in Holy Scripture, the biblical phase, repeated often by Jesus, "those who have ears to hear, let them hear," might be brought to mind by the idea of deafness, in the metaphorical sense of spiritual deafness.

Furthermore, because the city of Bath was famed for its water spots—baths, pools, and spas—a woman *beside Bath* might well suggest the woman *beside a well* whom Jesus met in Samaria, the woman who had such difficulty understanding Jesus' spiritual discourse. Just how appropriate this association may be is revealed later in the Wyf's own Prologue and Tale. The Wyf is further described as wrathful and proud; apparently prosperous in the weaving trade, she is conspicuously overdressed. As to her looks, we are told: "Bold was her face, fair, and all red of hue" (*CT* GP, 458), and we understand the origin of her truculent disposition; she is one in whom the humor of blood predominates and makes her a sanguine personality. Physiognomy reveals more of her character when the Narrator adds that she was "Gat-toothed," that is, there was a wide space between her two front teeth. While physiognomical manuals of the time interpreted a red face as indicating an angry, immodest nature drawn to drunkenness, the same manuals interpreted gat-teeth as indicating a sensual, irreverent, faithless nature.[1] The strategic placement of this physical detail right after a description of her amorous history drives home the point.

> Husbands she had had five within the Church,
> Not counting other company in youth,
> But we need not go into that right now.
> Three times she had been to Jerusalem,
> Many a strange stream had she crossed, indeed;
> At Rome she had been and at Bologna,
> At Compostela and at Cologne.
> She knew how to wander by the wayside!
> Gat-toothed she was, to tell the whole truth. (*CT* GP, 460–68)

The coupling of the descriptions of her pilgrimages and of her love-life presents her as a kind of sexual pilgrim eclectically passing

---

[1] There were many treatises on physiognomy existent in Chaucer's time, including the Pseudo-Aristotle *Secreta Secretorum*. An exhaustive treatment of Chaucer's use of physiognomical lore can be found in Walter Clyde Curry, *Chaucer and the Mediaeval Sciences* (London: George Allen & Unwin, 1960), especially chapters II, IV, V.

from one erotic partner to another, just as she amuses herself by visiting as many pilgrim sites as possible. The clearly ironic reference to "wandering by the wayside" thus governs both her spiritual and physical progress, in the same way that the physiognomical detail of her teeth reveals the inclination of her character. The added detail that she has had five husbands reaches back to the initial lines describing her as from "beside Bath" and illuminates the meaning of the reference; a woman nearby a body of water who is a bit hard of hearing and has had five husbands. Few in Chaucer's audience would have failed to make the association between the Wyf of Bath and the Samaritan woman at the well. Those who do fail need only wait until her Prologue when she herself refers directly to that biblical story.

However, as with so many of Chaucer's associations, this one plays with similitude and dissimilitude: The Wyf is like the Samaritan in that she has had five husbands and has difficulty understanding—the meaning of the figurative detail of being "a bit deaf." She is the exact contrary of the Samaritan in that the woman at the well whom Jesus tries to enlighten comes slowly to understand the truth and to proclaim it to her community; the Wyf of Bath remains stubbornly "deaf," persisting in believing whatever pleases her and excuses her excesses, and becomes a false preacher to her fellow pilgrims.

The Narrator completes his portrait of the Wyf with two further allusions the heavy irony of which is likely to have escaped him but not the literate audience: "Of the remedies of love she knew much, / For of that art she knew well the old dance" (*CT* GP, 475–46). Embedded here is a subtle but clear enough reference to Ovid and his comico-erotic works, the *Remedia Amoris (Remedies of Love)* and the *Ars Amatoria (Art of Love)*. The "Old Dance" is a timeless obscene reference to fornication that Chaucer uses frequently.

7 Canterbury Tales

WYF OF BATH'S PROLOGUE

THE ENTIRE PORTRAIT, employing physiognomy, biblical allusion, and intertextual reference, creates the sense of a character deeply marked by sensual appetite and willfulness, and it is this sense that is confirmed when the Wyf speaks for herself in her Prologue and Tale:

> Experience, though no authority
> Were in existence, is enough for me
> To tell of the woe that is in marriage;
> For you see, sirs, since I was twelve years old,
> Five husbands have I had in married state,
> (Thanks be to God Almighty and on high,
> That I have been able to wed so many).
>   (*Wyf of Bath's* Prologue [*WBP*], 1–7)

Mediaeval thinkers were generally in agreement that the way human beings come to know what they know—how we achieve intellectual understanding—is a dual process: What they identified as "authority" and "experience." The latter, called *experimentum* in the Latin used by mediaeval philosophers, brings us knowledge of the particulars of the physical world through the five senses; we learn, for instance, that fire is hot by touching, that is we *experiment*.

There are, however, many things that we cannot "experience" physically and directly, and these things include intellectual concepts, past historical events, and universals. We know, for instance, that Boethius wrote the *Consolation of Philosophy* and that Jesus met a Samaritan by a well, not through our personal experience, but through the authority of the traditions and texts that tell us so.

Complete and valid human knowledge requires both experience and authority. Although authority is the vehicle of more purely intellectual knowledge and experience the vehicle of more concrete, physical, particular knowledge, together they form a harmonious union designed to bring mankind to holistic truth.

The fact that the Wyf divides authority from experience and rejects authority as unnecessary to her understanding of marriage is the principal trope by which she is to be understood: She personifies divisiveness and fragmentation. The Wyf of Bath pulls asunder everything that is meant to be united, beginning with experience and authority but reaching well beyond to everything in her life. She divides her husbands into good and bad: Three were "good" in handing authority over to her, but "bad" in that they were old and impotent; two were "good" in the experience of sex, but "bad" in resisting her authority over them. Thus she separates sex from love, never able to unite the two; she divorces old age from youth and thus fragments her own life into her "good" youth and her despised old age; she splinters sign from signified in consistently deforming the meaning of the texts she quotes to prove the opposite of what the authors of those texts intended.

It is with considerable irony that Chaucer presents the Wyf as a polemical figure who conducts her diatribe against authority entirely by reliance on authority itself, invoking the most important and influential of philosophers and theologians and their works. Her goal in everything she says is self-justification. In response to the biblical and theological texts that declare that widows should remain widows and not remarry, she fashions an exegesis that erases their lesson or twists the texts to make them say the opposite of what, in fact, they say. As for all relativists, words mean what the Wyf wants them to mean.

> But I was told, indeed, not long ago,
> That since Christ went once and only the once
> To wedding, in Cana of Galilee,
> That I, too, should only be wedded once
> ....
> Beside a well, Jesus, God and man
> Spoke in reproach of the Samaritan
> "Thou hast had five husbands," so said he,
> And that very man that now hath thee
> Is not thy husband,' said he certainly.
> But what he meant by that I cannot say. (*WBP*, 9–20)

Claiming not to understand the text, the Wyf goes on to argue with it sophistically: Why should the fifth not be legitimate? How many could she have had? Where is there written a definition of the exact number anyway? Dismissing both New Testament accounts, the Wyf reveals her personal preference:

> But one thing I know, clearly and truly
> God bade us to go wax and multiply;
> Ah! that sweet text I can well understand. (*WBP*, 28–30)

Just as she divides experience from authority and sex from love, here the Wyf divorces the New Testament from the Old Testament, fragmenting the book that, for Christians, is a mystical integration of parts into a sacred whole. Throughout her Prologue, the Wyf reveals more about herself than she intends, and an ironic gap opens up between what she intends by her words and what the audience perceives. Her understanding, as she admits, is limited to the Old Covenant. Here and throughout the Prologue and Tale, Chaucer, with superb irony, identifies the Wyf with all that is "old." As she continues her biography, we learn that what the Wyf hates and most fears is old age, and this identification of the self with the very thing she hates reveals her as a victim, not of patriarchal society as some have suggested, but of self-contradiction and self-loathing.

In addition to the psychological manipulation of the idea of old age, Chaucer has, as well, employed several literary models for the Wyf, the main one being La Vieille (the old bawd) from the *Romance of the Rose*, a bitter, cynical creature who laments the loss of her youth and beauty, but who purports to teach the young sexual skills. The tradition of the old bawd signifies at the psychological level a kind of schizophrenic severing of the present from the past and a morbid nostalgia for what was, an imagined youth where all was bliss. At the textual level, the same dichotomy is referred to as the fleshly sense and the spiritual sense. Metaphorically the tradition represents the old as all that lacks the spiritual: body without soul, the letter of the law without the spirit of the law, sex without love, sign without signified. One of the most powerful and influential uses of the metaphor of old and new is St. Paul's instruction to us, "That ye put off concerning the former conversation the old man. . . . And that ye put on the new man (Ephesians 4:22, 24).

This same metaphoric contrast between old and new is found, as well, in the mediaeval concept of the written text as consisting of two parts, or levels—the literal and the symbolic. The text was made analogous to the human being who consists of body and soul, and its corresponding parts were the letter—the literal level of the written words—and the spirit—the meaning of the words and sentences. Again, St. Paul: "For the letter killeth, but the spirit giveth life" (II Corinthians 3:6) and, "that we should serve in the newness of the spirit, and not in the oldness of the letter" (Romans 7: 6). The analogy was regularly extended in the Middle Ages from body and soul to Old and New Testaments, to the Synagogue and the Church, to the particular and the universal, the literal and the symbolic. In all of these uses of the metaphor, what is commended is the unity of the parts within the whole.

Chaucer's brilliance in the creation of the Wyf was to have personified in a single character so many of the senses of the figura of the old, and to have done so in a humorous yet instructive way. Even in her championing of old texts, the Wyf is still a divider, for while she may prefer Genesis to the Gospels, she has "waxed" plenty but not "multiplied." With all the detail of her five marriages and other "company," there is never mention of children, and we are left with the impression that despite her vigorous appetite, she is without fertility; just as her words lack truth, her sexuality lacks fruit. And, as she does with New Testament texts she invokes, the Wyf half-quotes her favorite verses from Genesis, muzzling the main idea: "and they shall be one flesh" (Genesis 2:24).

Again she quotes a Gospel (Matthew 19:5) only to turn it on its head:

> I know quite well that He said my husband
> Should leave mother and father and be mine,
> But He never did say how many should!
> No talk of bigamy or octogomy. (*WBP*, 30–33)

Feigning inability to comprehend the spirit of the text, she clings to its letter, and once again disparagingly compares this New Testament text to another from the Old Testament. What about King Solomon, he had a lot more wives than one? I wish, she cries, I could be "refreshed" half so often as he!

The Wyf of Bath, whose name is given as both Alys (*WBP*, 320) and Alisoun (*WBP*, 804), has a particular penchant for the writings of St. Paul who had much to say about marriage, chastity, and love. One might imagine that Paul's teaching on these subjects would be distinctly unpalatable to the lusty Wyf, but she has no problem with what the Apostle, as she calls him, intended in his writings because, with sophistical agility, she simpy deforms his message. "For it is better to marry than to burn" (I Corinthians 7:9) becomes for Alys encouragement to marry six or even more men, despite Paul's preceding verse urging widows to remain in widowhood, which she conveniently ignores. In dealing with St. Paul, the Wyf's methodology is always to half-quote:

> My husband shall have it both night and day
> When he wants to pay the debt he owes me.
> Yes, husbands I shall have, make no mistake—
> And he shall be my debtor and my slave,
> And have his tribulation there withal
> Upon his flesh, while I remain his wife.
> I have the power during all my life
> Over his own body, and he does not.
> Just so the Apostle told it to me,
> And ordered our husbands to love us well.
> Now there's a text I find delightful! (*WBP*, 152–62)

The Pauline text that Alys is taking apart and selectively quoting is this:

> Let the husband render unto his wife due benevolence
> (*debitum*, or debt in the Latin): *and likewise, the wife*
> *unto the husband.*
> The wife hath not power over her own body, but the husband: and likewise also the husband hath not power over his own body, but the wife.
> Defraud ye not one the other, except it be with consent for a time, that ye may give yourselves to fasting and prayer.
> (I Corinthians 7:3–5, my emphasis)

The mutual obedience of husband and wife that Paul preaches is turned by Alys into the oppression of the man by the woman. The harmony of the married couple who have sacramentally become as one body is turned into the discord and tyranny of master and slave.

Second only to St. Paul in the Wyf's list of useful authors comes St. Jerome, and especially his tract *Adversus Jovinianum*, in which the saint rebuts the ideas of the heretical monk, Jovinian. Indeed, as her polemic advances, Alys begins to emerge as an avatar of the heterodox Jovinian, arguing against the orthodox Jerome. Jovinian published a number of controversial and even heretical ideas that might be summarized as relativistic. He maintained that there are no degrees of merit nor of reward, and that all those souls who gain heaven reside there in the same state; he asserted that all who are baptized are immune from the devil; and, the idea that excited Alys's interest, he claimed that there were no degrees of goodness between virginity, the married state, and widowhood, that is to say, one was as good as another.

The wife's motto throughout the polemic over spiritual perfection seems to be "Aim Low!" St. Jerome maintained that while marriage is not only a good and even a sacrament instituted by Christ, virginity is a different and greater good, and that widowhood is similar to virginity. The oft-married Alys agrees with Jerome's argument, but with skillful sophistry turns it around to her own purposes:

> Virginity is a great perfection,
> So is continence combined with prayer.
> But Christ who of perfection is the well
> Bade not everyone that they go and sell
> All that they had and give it to the poor
> And in that way follow in His footsteps.
> He spoke to those who would live perfectly,
> And that, by George, sirs, is surely not I! (*WBP*, 105–12)

She continues her disquisition on *Adversus Jovinianum* taking the side of the heretic and posing Jovinian's rhetorical question:

> And by the way, tell me, too, to what end
> Were our genitalia so constructed,
> And by so perfectly wise a maker?
> For surely they were not made for nothing!
> So gloss as you will and swear up and down
> That they are only for purgation of
> Urine, and that our little things are there

> Just so to tell a female from a male,
> And for no other reason—say you not!
> By experience we know otherwise. (*WBP,* 115–24)

Having turned her authoritative texts upside down, the Wyf returns to her biography and describes her various husbands. As a champion of female sovereignty and a voice for feminism, Alys does as poor a job as she did as theological apologist. In her temerity and self-congratulation in being aggressive and dominant, the Wyf articulates and validates most of the complaints against women in the mediaeval misogynist tradition—a largely literary tradition built on defamations of woman's character. Thus she bluntly declares, "There is no man who can half so boldly / Lie and swear as we women can" (*WBP,* 227–28). She goes on to admit marrying for money, of cheating on her husbands, of browbeating them, and of blackmailing them for their wealth by withholding sex; ever divisive, she comodifies sex and declares to her old husbands, "Though thou go mad, thou shalt not ever be / Master of both my body and my goods!" (*WBP,* 313–14)

Because for her there is no universal Love in which human erotic experience participates, Alys has no qualms about sexual extortion, just as she does not blush to deceive and humiliate her husbands. Marriage is a war in which husand and wife are enemies, and the stronger comes to dominate the weaker. As a pragmatist, the Wyf emphasizes experience because it is only in the present moment that sensual pleasure can occur, and desire and its satisfaction are what are worth living for. The bitter irony of such a psychology is that while the present is all that matters, it ceases to exist when carved off from the past and the future, an irony dramatized in the persona of the Wyf.

The portrait of the Wyf of Bath is not, however, relentlessly negative, nor does she appear as purely cynical. Chaucer portrays her with considerable subtlety, and she is one of the few characters to exhibit genuine pathos. Although, as she boasts, she treats others as things and uses people to satisfy her desires, Alys does not emerge as a villain because her true victim is herself. In her long, nostalgic recollection of her past, there are two remarkable passages in which the Wyf reveals the depth of her sadness:

> But—Oh, Lord Christ!—whenever I look back
> Upon my youth and on my joie de vivre,
> It stirs me to the bottom of my heart,
> Oh yes indeed, it does my heart such good
> That I have had my world within my time.
> Old age, alas, that poisons everything,
> Has robbed me of my beauty and my strength.
> So go! Farewell! To hell with everything!
> The flower is gone, what more can I say?
> The bran I'll try to peddle, as I may.
> And so to be happy, I will pretend. (*WBP*, 469–79)

Through this lament Chaucer's identification of the Wyf with La Vieille of the *Romance of the Rose* takes on greater meaning. Like her literary predecessor, the Wyf is oldness itself. Psychologically the Wyf's existential reality is fixed in the past and in the future, and her happiness is restricted to nostalgic memory and voluptuous anticipation, a state completely at odds with her philosophy of present experience. Just as she has separated every other unity, Alys has fragmented the course of her own existence, divorcing present from past and present from future, leaving no center to her life, no present point from which she can integrate the past with the future in the Augustinian sense of lived time. Instead, she abides in memory and imagination, glorifying herself in her biographical Prologue through a recollected and reconstructed past, as well as fantastically transforming herself from old to young in her imaginary Tale, as we will see. As she herself exclaims, only by "pretending" (*fonde, WBP*, 479, from *fynden*, fabricate), can she find happiness.

In another passage of long, rambling reminiscence and self-aggrandizement, Alys stops short and pitifully exclaims, "Alas, Alas!

That love was ever sin!" (*WBP*, 614). The pathetic misconception that love is sinful is the result of the perverse separation of physical love from spiritual love, or as Augustine put it, divorcing love of the created from love of the Creator. When Augustine said, "Love, and do as you will,"[1] he indicated the integrating power of *Agape*, or Charity, that unites and harmonizes the other forms of love, friendship and eros, into a whole in which the will is properly directed. Alys's outburst identifying love as sin is the precise opposite of Augustine's salvific view of love.

The *Wyf of Bath*'s Prologue is the longest in the collection and her Tale one of the shortest, suggesting that, perhaps, Chaucer has lost control of the structure and let the Prologue go on too long, the Tale not long enough. However, this very imbalance suggests another possible literary effect—that the inversion of length of Prologue and of Tale is a meaningful "error" calling for a correction through which we realize that the Wyf's highly biographical Prologue is her Tale, to which the very brief Tale could serve as Prologue. Such an inversion would be in keeping with all the other inversions and distortions that Alisoun has performed. From the perception of this structure, we further realize that the Prologue and Tale are really one and the same: the Prologue being a self-flattering reminiscence in which fantasy plays a major part, the Tale being a fairyland fantasy in which biography plays a major part.

---

[1] *The seventh homily on the Letter of John*, section 8.

8 Canterbury Tales

THE WYF OF BATH'S TALE

ALISOUN SETS her Tale in the distant past, "In the olden days of King Arthur" (*Wyf of Bath's Tale [WBT]*, 857), an ideal world, she thinks, because it was a "fairyland," full of fantastic beings and wondrous happenings. This, Alisoun editorializes, has been quite ruined by the arrival of Christianity. Whereas in the good old days a woman could count on being sexually assaulted by an imp or two hiding in the bushes, now the Church has chased away these spirits:

> For now where once there walked about an elf,
> There walks the holy friar all by himself,
> All the morning long, right up until noon,
> Mumbling his matins and other prayers,
> Meandering through his territory.
> Women may now go safely up and down!
> In every bush and under every tree,
> There is no other incubus but he. (*WBT*, 873–80)

Disappointed with the contemporary world in which the Church outlaws sexual assault upon women, the Wyf tells a tale about rape in which she constructs a fantasyland where all desires, no matter how unlikely, come true. The hero, a lusty young knight the author calls him, encounters a young woman walking alone and rapes her. Brought before the King, the rapist receives the death penalty, as the law of the land provides. However, the Queen "and all the ladies" intercede for him, and the King eventually abdicates his power and responsibility to his wife.

This narrative element creates a sharp contrast between male justice and female justice, for whereas male justice, represented by the King, would have punished an assault upon a woman with the harshest penalty, female justice, represented by the Queen, merely assigns the rapist a didactic riddle: "What is it that women most desire?" Only if he fails to find the correct answer will the King's original sentence be carried out. This leniency toward sexual violence echoes, of course, the author's own preference for the rough-and-ready days of erotic lawlessness and an imp in every bush, and she is thus identified with one of her own characters, the Queen.

Chaucer perfected the device of having the fictional author project herself, or himself, into the tale in such a way that he or she reveals something of the self without intending to. Thus in Chaucer's hands, this is a device creating irony. He employs it widely in the *Canterbury Tales* as a means of undermining certain characters and satirizing their motives. In none of the Tales is it used more extensively than in the Wyf's. Just as the Queen in wresting power from her husband and taking control of the young knight is a projection of Alisoun's desire to dominate men, so, too, considering our author's confessed attraction to lawless sex, the raped maiden is also a projection of Alys's fantasies. These, as we will see, are not the end of the author's self-fashionings in her Tale.

The Knight sets out to find the answer to the riddle and in the process of describing his quest Alisoun manages to trot out again virtually every accusation against women in the misogynist tradition: Some from whom he seeks the answer to the riddle say that women most desire riches, some say honors, others suggest amusements, rich clothing, sex. But, according to Alys, the one that got closest to the truth, albeit without actually hitting on it, was whoever proposed that what women most desire is "flattery" (*WBT*, 925–34). The omniscient author develops her opinion:

> A man shall win us best with flattery,
> Lots of attention and much indulgence.
> By such devices we are snared for sure.
> Some others said that what we loved best
> Was to be free and do as we right pleased,
> And that no one name our vices to us,
> But call us wise, perfect in every way.
> For sure it is that there is none of us,
> Should someone try to throw it in our face,
> Who will not strike him for telling the truth! (*WBT*, 932–41)

Realizing the inadequacy of these answers (we know not how), the hopeless Knight dejectedly rides home to his fate but happens on the way to perceive in a clearing in the woods a group of twenty-four fairies dancing in a ring. As he approaches them, the lovely ladies disappear, and all that is left in their place is—a wyf! Alys describes this creature in most unflattering terms, calling her "the foulest being ever seen," and emphasizes her "oldness." The old hag offers to reveal the answer to the riddle if the knight promises to grant her whatever she requires. She guarantees the Knight that she and the Queen are of the same mind (*WBT*, 1016). This allusion of similitude to the Queen suggests even further forms of transmogrification, and we begin to suspect that in this land of shape-shifting, the Old Wyf may be the Queen herself in disguise. We recall that the Tale opens with a reference to the magical days when the elf-queen and her fairy retinue "danced on many a green," and that the Knight comes upon such a group dancing upon a "greene."

If the old hag is a manifestation of the Queen, we realize that the Queen herself is giving the Knight the answer to the riddle she has assigned him. If, in addition, the Queen is a projection of the author, then the hag is as well. However, it is not only through the device of magic that the audience is led to identify the hag with the Wyf of Bath, but also through the unmistakable similarity of psychology.

Alisoun's greatest preoccupation in life is growing old. It is only age, she believes, that prevents her from bringing together the two things she most desires—power and sex. Although she had power over her first three husbands, they were, she claims, sexually inadequate. Although she had a vigorous sex life with her two younger husbands, her power over them was limited. Now, looking for a sixth husband, she fears that her advancing age will frustrate her desire to find a spirited young man over whom, however, she can maintain control.

Is it surprising, then, that such an author's imagination creates a fairyland world where all one's wishes come true? The Old Hag supplies the correct answer to the riddle and the Knight saves his life, but he must now grant the Old Wyf's wish, which, she reveals, is that he marry her:

> Great was the woe that the knight felt inside
> When he found himself in bed with that bride.
> He wept, he moaned, and he turned to and fro,
> But his old wyf lay smiling ear to ear
> And said unto him, "O my husband dear,
> Is this how big brave knights act with their wives?"
> (*WBT*, 1083–88)

After a long, philosophical speech on natural gentility, the Old Wyf creates still another conundrum for the harried Knight, telling him to choose whether he will have her faithful and ugly or beautiful and free to do as she pleases. We note in this development of the Tale another example of how fond our author is of dichotomies. The Knight, either through exhaustion or some kind of shrewd intuition, surrenders his power of choice to his Wyf, putting himself in her "wise governance," and, as it happens so often in fantasyland, he gets everything he might want:

"Have I, then, got mastery of you,
So that I have choice and power to rule?"
"Indeed, dear wyf," quod he, "I think that best."
"Kiss me," quod she, "for now we are as one,
For, by my word, I will be both to you,
That is, I will be both fair and faithful." (*WBT*, 1236–41)

In the imaginary world of Alisoun, set deep in the past but full of promise for the future, all of the binaries she has construed are reconciled to her advantage; she gains both power and sexual satisfaction, her youthful past becomes her ageless future, and finally, she has an authoritative text of her own making that represents experience as it ought to be.

But this is fantasy, and Alisoun must return to the "real" world of the Canterbury pilgrimage and her fragmented life, and that return, as we see in her conclusion, is accompanied by the same strange combination of wishful thinking of her Tale and the aggressive and bitter emotions of her Prologue:

So they lived happily to their lives' end
In perfect joy; may Jesus Christ us send
Husbands all meek, and young, and good in bed,
And the grace to outlive all those we wed;
Also I pray Christ to cut short the lives
 Of men who won't be governed by their wives,
And all old men, and all angry misers,
Let God send them soon every pestilence! (*WBT*, 1257–64)

9   Canterbury Tales

THE PARDONER'S PROLOGUE

HE PARDONER, the Wyf's fellow pilgrim, has inter-rupted her during her Prologue, encouraging her to continue her diatribe because he had been going to marry, but from her description of the experience, he was now rethinking the decision. He is the personification of irony at its most contemptuous. Having caught the Wyf's error in attributing a scriptural quotation of St. John to St. Mark, the Pardoner sneeringly blurts out: "Madame, by God and by Saint John! / You are a first rate preacher in all this!" (*WBP*, 164–65), smirking, we assume, at those other pilgrims, such as the Nun's Priest, who were sufficiently educated to perceive the Wyf's error and the Pardoner's sarcasm.

Pardoners were professional fundraisers hired by religious institutions and by bishops to sell indulgences and pardons for various moral offenses in order to raise money for charitable endeavors. These pardoners, who were often, but not always, clerics, seem to have derived their income by taking a percentage of the monies they raised. The possibility of abuse of such powers is too obvious to need spelling out, and history makes clear that in Chaucer's time the abuse was extensive.

In the case of the Wyf of Bath, we have seen that Chaucer's method of characterization was to single out a particular characteristic and make of it a "topos," that is, a motif from which the delineation of the character and the construction of meaning flow. Alisoun's "topos" was old age.

In the case of the Pardoner, the single element of his portrait from which all other characteristics draw significance is his sexual impotence. Seen by many as a eunuch and by others as a passive homosexual, the Pardoner is a study in a multitude of forms of impotence. The Narrator is uncharacteristically blatant in his description of the Pardoner in the General Prologue:

> This Pardoner's hair was yellow like wax,
> And it hung down flat like a clump of flax,
> In little strands hung the hairs that he had,
> And he spread them all across his shoulders;
> Thin they laid, one tress after another.
> But no hood wore he, so to look *tres chic*,
> For he had stuffed it into his wallet.
> He thought this get-up was the newest fashion.
> Bare headed, except for a cap, he rode.
> His eyes were gleaming, just like a hare's.
> On the cap he had a holy picture.
> He rode with his wallet between his legs,
> Stuffed fat with pardons, coming hot from Rome.
> A voice he had on him as high as a goat's.
> No beard had he, nor would he ever have;
> As smooth he was as if he had just shaved.
> I thought he was a eunuch or a queer. (*CT* GP, 675–91)

Like most of the descriptions of the General Prologue, this one reveals not only the physical appearance of the character but, through metaphorizing physical characteristics, it manifests the inner self. The Pardoner has yellow-white hair and bright pink, rabbit-like eyes. His hair is thin, and he has arranged it, strand by strand, so as to have it fan across his shoulders. The picture is already grotesque, bespeaking weakness and debility, but when the Narrator adds that he had a voice as high as a goat's, this detail brings all the others into focus, and we see the character—just as does the Narrator—as a eunuch, or homosexual, or both.

The Pardoner's sexuality has long been recognized as the chief clue to his significance, a significance generally seen as malevolent. Indeed, many agree with the great Chaucer scholar G. L. Kittredge that the Pardoner is "the one lost soul" on the pilgrimage.[1] His declaration to the Wyf of Bath that he was about to be married is seen as an attempt to mask his homosexuality and, from this need, some deduce a psychology of self-hatred. Again, the Narrator makes this disturbingly clear in the General Prologue when he describes the company the Pardoner keeps:

> This Summoner bore to him a stiff burden,
> No trumpet ever made such a great noise. (*CT* GP, 673–64)

The Pardoner, whose voice, we know, is high, has been singing the popular song, "Come hither, love, to me!" (*CT* GP, 672), and the Summoner is accompanying him as the bass, providing what was called the *cantus firmus* or "stif bourdoun." The provocative phrase, *bore him a stiff burden,* strongly suggests a scatological pun identifying the Pardoner as a passive homosexual partnered up with the Summoner, who, himself, is hideously described in the General Prologue as debauched and probably syphilitic.

Beyond the psychological, the Pardoner looms as a powerful intellectual who seeks to demonstrate his superiority over his fellow pilgrims, as well as his disdain for them, by using language in such a rhetorically seductive way that he can warn them that he intends to deceive them, show them exactly how he will do it, and still get away with it. His is a kind of demonic daring of intellectual pride. If we seek the Pardoner's motivation, we find that it is, like all motivations, psychological; his self-loathing is projected as a virulent hatred for his fellow man. But his elaborate project of

---

[1] George L. Kittredge, *Chaucer and His Poetry* (Cambridge, MA: Harvard University Press, 1970), 180.

deception reveals far more than his motives; it reveals the inevitable morbidity of the view that language constructs reality, and that words are all there is.

Like Pandarus, though far more sinister, the Pardoner occupies a ghastly world deprived of all that is vigorous and life-affirming, and the sign of this deadliness is sexual impotence, a sign signifying not only the debility of the body, but of the intellect and spirit, as well. The Pardoner's words, like his manhood, are without issue; his sexuality is disconnected from life, his words disconnected from truth.

Like the Wyf of Bath, the Pardoner produces a highly biographical Prologue to his short, splendid Tale consisting largely of a frank confessional account of his exploitation of the poor and ignorant. It is all about language ill-used. A great rhetorician, the Pardoner uses words and signs of all kinds to lure his churchgoing audience: From the pulpit he waves papal bulls of indulgence and his Bishop's seal (*Pardoner's* Prologue [*PP*], 336–67); he spices up his sermon with phrases in Latin so as to awe the crowd (*PP*, 344–46); then he unveils his collection of relics:

> Then show I forth my long crystal boxes,
> Stuffed with old rags and full of old bones—
> Relics they be, or so they all believe. (*PP*, 347–79)

In the Pardoner's worldview it is human believing, knowing, and naming that give reality to the intelligible—subjective credence *(wenyng)* that quickens the object of belief. Itemizing the phony relics that he carries and describing other low tricks he uses to get money from the poor, the Pardoner boasts that in this way he has earned a small fortune. He is blatant concerning his motivation:

> My goal is to get money for myself,
> In no way is it to correct their sins.
> As far as I care, when they are buried,
> Their souls can go picking blackberries! (*PP*, 403–6)

More and more daring, the Pardoner goes further in his long confession, articulating through his life's motto the motto that will govern his Tale. In so doing, he comes dangerously close to revealing the true nature of his evil:

> For covetousness I preach, only that,
> And so my theme is now and always was,
> *Radix malorum est cupiditas.*
> This way I can preach against the same vice
> That I practice, and that is avarice. (*PP*, 424–28)

Like his announced intention to marry, the Pardoner's confession of his sins appears to be something of a smoke screen. Not that he is not avaricious, lustful, dishonest, and cynical—he is; but there is something far more malevolent than even these serious vices, and it is something that he intends to keep hidden. Hatred.

In order that the Pardoner succeed in duping his fellow pilgrims, he must try to convince them that, although a rogue, he is congenial. After all, he is candid; he does his best to entertain them; despite his appearance, he acts like one of them, a member of the community. Were his pilgrim audience to sense that the Pardoner despises them as much as he hates himself, that, indeed, he is a life-hater incarnate, he would have no chance of deceiving them.

His motto, characterizing the Pardoner's life and Tale is, however, valid, and is an example of the potential for ambiguity within language. There is a certain irony in the fact that when this phrase, from I Timothy 6:10, was translated into English, it became: "For money is the root of all evil," a limited meaning of the Latin *cupiditas*, and the one the Pardoner would have us accept. But Chaucer, who had received a Catholic education, would have known, not only the range of meanings of the word in Latin, but also its Augustinian theology: *Cupiditas* is all disordered desire, an illustration of the Bishop of Hippo's theory of use and enjoyment that contends that lower or limited goods are to be *used* in order to reach and to *enjoy* the higher. Unlike the puritanical view that money and all material things are evil, Chaucer is likely to have held the dominant mediaeval Catholic view that the world and everything in it, including money, are good—as long as they assume their proper place in a well-ordered moral hierarchy of goods and desires.

Because he is a figure of perversity, the Pardoner's hierarchy of goods is disordered, and that perverse disorder is reflected in his treatment of signs. He is a character preoccupied with signs and committed to preventing them from signifying anything real or true. In mediaeval epistemology, several distinct categories of sign were recognized. According to Augustine, who was the principal philosopher of language in the Middle Ages and one of Chaucer's most important sources, the two basic kinds of sign are the natural sign and the conventional sign. Natural signs are those that are independent of human intention, such as smoke, which signifies fire, and animal tracks, the sign of an animal's passage. The most important kind of conventional sign is words, for these signs are created through the cultural "agreement" of a given community that a certain sign shall stand for a certain thing or idea. This explains the difference of words for the same thing from one language group, or community, to another.[2]

Words, like all conventional signs, depend on the intention of the speaker, and as Augustine shows, ambiguity is created when the intention of the speaker and the words he speaks differ. When we use a sign for a thing to signify something other than is conventionally signified, we have created either a metaphor or an ambiguity; a resultant ambiguity may be irony, or it may be the lie. In the case of the Pardoner, his intention in using words is not to communicate their conventional meaning, nor to create beautiful metaphors or amusing ambiguities; it is to create false meaning so as to conceal his intention and beguile his listeners.

---

2 St. Augustine, *On Christian Doctrine,* II, i. ed. and trans. D. W. Robertson (New York: Liberal Arts Press, 1958).

The Pardoner's molestation of language is not, however, limited to conventional signs. His is an unlimited assault on signification itself, beginning with the relation of word to thing, intensifying with the separation of the relic from the whole of which it is a part, and culminating in the deicidal sacrilege of denying the *mysterium* of presence in the consecrated Host. In the process of his Prologue and his Tale the Pardoner invokes every category of sign recognized in mediaeval Christian thought in order to undermine each one successively.[3]

The range of signification in the Pardoner's Prologue and Tale reflects the gamut of the sign in mediaeval thought: The word, most familiar of all signs, bears to its signified a conventional relation; the relic and that which it betokens, unlike the word and its meaning, is a natural sign in that the relic, in order to have any signifying power at all, must be an actual part of that which it signifies (in rhetorical terms, it is like a synecdoche); the consecrated Host is unique in that it is the only example in its class, a category in which the sign and the signified are ontologically exactly the same.

The Pardoner's misuse of words is matched, if not trumped, by his misuse of relics. He is attracted to relics, one suspects, because of their materiality. Unlike words, which are abstract and ephemeral, the relic is at one and the same time *res* and *signum*, and it is its physical participation in the thing, not its conventional relation to it as sign, that creates its miraculous power. Usually a part of the body of a saint or a physical object that has touched the body of the saint, the relic's representational power depends completely on its physical contiguity with the whole of which it is a part.

The Pardoner's misuse of relics is not only a gambit to cheat the ignorant, it is a deconstruction of the relic through redefining its ontology as purely subjective and residing in the devotee. For him, the power of the relic, if any, arises in the belief of the faithful who

---

[3] I have developed this idea more extensively in "*Lo how I vanysshe*: the Pardoner's War on Signs," in *Chaucer and Language* (Montreal: McGill-Queen's University Press, 2002).

venerate the object. Such subjectivism has several consequences for the theory of signs because if a thing (or word) is simply what one wants it to be or if its virtue arises out of the confidence or sentiment of the human observer, then any sign will do; if we all agree to call dogs cats, then we have acceptable signification. Similarly, according to the relativist, if we agree that a newly woven piece of cloth is a piece of the sail of St. Peter's ship, then it is!

Physicality also characterizes the sensational metaphoricity of the Pardoner, but unlike the relic that brings back to life the whole of which it is part, the Pardoner's use of the body and body parts—particularly digestive passages and orifices—degrades and annihilates:

> O paunch! o belly, o stinking guts,
> Full of dung and of corruption!
> At both ends of you the sound is foul.
> (*Pardoner's Tale* [*PT*], 534–36)

Here the human body is reduced to its digestive tract, the mouth associated with the rectum, and the whole projected as a cosmology of dissolution and defecation in which language, which issues from the mouth is identified with the feces that issue from the lower orifice. Expressing more than he realizes, the Pardoner now begins to reveal through his metaphors the fecal world that he inhabits. Having abused and degraded words as well as relics in his Prologue, the Pardoner now takes the final step in his war on signs in his Tale by making its controlling metaphor one of transubstantiation.

10 Canterbury Tales

THE PARDONER'S TALE

FOUND IN NUMEROUS cultures in various versions throughout the world,[1] the Tale is a masterpiece of fiction that derives its impact from *peripeteia*, or ironic reversal. The economic narrative—just over 500 lines—features three young "riotours," men who indulge in gluttony, swearing, drunkenness, and a variety of other sensual excesses. Told by a young boy that Death has taken away one of their companions, the three swear an oath to find Death and slay him.

The three are thus swiftly characterized as sensualists, materialists, and literalists, guilty of the abuses of intellect and body, and, significantly, practitioners of the same vices that their author has admitted to in his Prologue. The fact that the child who brings the news of the death to them uses personification and metaphoric discourse to describe the plague that has killed many, calling death a "sneaky thief" who "slays with his spear," seems to echo St. Paul's famous description of human understanding: "When I was a child, I spake as a child, I thought as a child: but when I became a man, I put away childish things. For now we see through a glass darkly: but then, face to face." (I Corinthians 13:11–12). Paul's immortal

---

[1] Versions of the story are found throughout Europe, Asia, and Africa. A modern version of it can be seen in the 1948 Humphrey Bogart film, *Treasure of the Sierra Madre*.

verses address the relation of language to understanding and characterize initial speaking and comprehension as a kind of intellectual childhood marked by subjectivity—gazing in a mirror—that gives way, or should, to a maturity in which one comes to know "even as I am known," that is, objectively.

The three young sensualists adopt the metaphoric concept of death used by the child and literalize it, setting out to find this "false traitor, Death" (*Pardoner's Tale* [*PT*], 699). We are reminded here of St. Augustine's warning concerning the seriousness of the abuse of language, in which one takes the literal as metaphoric and the metaphoric as literal:

> For at the outset you must be very careful lest you take figurative expressions literally. What the Apostle says applies to this problem: "For the letter killeth, but the spirit quickeneth." That is, when what is said figuratively is taken as though it were literal, it is understood carnally. Nor can anything more appropriately be called the death of the soul than that condition in which the thing that distinguishes us from the beast, which is the understanding, is subjected to the flesh in the pursuit of the letter. (*De doctrina Christiana* III, v)

This is precisely what the three characters created by the Pardoner do just as its opposite, which Augustine also warns against—taking the literal as figurative—is what the Pardoner himself does with relics. In their quest, the three young thugs encounter an old, wizened man, who, by his appearance, they associate with death. They are right in this, as the old man's complaint reveals:

> "Death, alas, does not want to take my life,
> And so I wander like a restless waif,
> And on the ground that is my mother's door,
> I knock with my staff, all day and all night,
> Crying, 'O dear Mother, please let me in!'
> Low! How I vanish, flesh and blood and skin!" (*PT*, 727–32)

Convinced that the old man is in league with Death, the three youths constrain him to show them where Death abides. He obliges by pointing to a "crooked way" (*PT*, 761) at the end of which, he states, they will find Death under an oak tree. The sensational dénouement begins when the trio arrives at the oak—an ancient symbol of death—and finds a mass of gold coins scattered on the ground at the roots of the tree. The iconography of the scene brilliantly echoes the Pardoner's motto, "the root of all evil is money," and combines it with another scriptural warning, "the wages of sin is death" (Romans 6:23).

The eldest of this infernal trinity sends the youngest to town to fetch "bread and wine" to celebrate their good fortune. He then plots with the other member of the "brotherhood" to murder the youngest when he returns, so as to divide the treasure by two rather than three. The youngest is no less malicious and plots to kill both of his partners upon his return. The way the Pardoner has him plan this reveals the spirit of his authorship:

> For this was utterly his firm intent
> To murder them both, nor ever repent.
> And so off he went, he didn't tarry,
> Right to town to the apothecary,
> And he told him what he wanted to buy,
> Some poison to kill a pack of rats with. (*PT*, 849–54)

Upon his return the youth is murdered and his killers celebrate by eating the bread and drinking the poisoned wine that he brought them. In this ironic way they finally meet the Death they had set out to find.

The way in which Chaucer has constructed his retelling of this widespread story is far more philosophical than any of its predecessors. Chaucer's use of eucharistic symbolism is insistent. The description of the discovery of the lucre as a "grace" (*PT*, 783) and the fetching of bread and wine to celebrate it obviously evoke sacramental associations. The fact that the youngest of the trio carries these salvific elements to his waiting brothers ironically echoes the liturgical theme *"Benedictus qui venit in nomine Domini,"* which is said in the traditional Catholic Mass as part of the *Sanctus* that immediately precedes the transubstantiation of the bread and wine into the body and blood of Jesus.

As with his many other religious signs, the Pardoner perverts all this, directing the symbols of salvation toward death and damnation. Moreover, the use of Eucharistic allusions reaches beyond the symbolic and the didactic to become specific commentary regarding one of the gravest social problems of Chaucer's time.

Dubbed "Lollards," it is thought because they resentfully mumbled orthodox Christian prayers (*lollen,* to mumble), these English proto-Protestants adopted Chaucer's contemporary, John Wyclif, as their theological spokesman. Wyclif was a priest and Oxford professor of theology who attacked the Church in numerous ways, including, late in his career, by his denial of the truth of transubstantiation.

The Pardoner's references to bread and rats, wine and poison, were likely to strike a sharp chord with his audience since they are allusions to Lollard polemics against orthodox believers. "What," they taunted, "if a rat or mouse were to get to the consecrated Host in the ciborium during the night, and eat it? Would the rat have received the Body and Blood of Jesus Christ? Would the sacrament work its power on the rat, giving it eternal life?" These were some of the degrading considerations used to ridicule the Catholic belief in transubstantiation, and beyond that, any sacramental transformation. Here the Pardoner seems actually to be borrowing directly from Wyclif's own necrotic imagery as he creates the dénouement of his story, for it is Wyclif who wrote: "The sacrament of the altar is bread, but naturally considered it is worse than rat food; the sacrament of the chalice is wine, but naturally considered it is worse than poison."[2]

---

[2] John Wyclif, *De apostasia,* ed. Michael Djiewicki, in *Wyclif's Latin Works* (London: Trübner, for the Wyclif Society, 1889), vol. 9, 172.

The echo of this lugubrious language is loud in the Pardoner's description of the transformation of life into death that the three rioters undergo. As we have seen, the youngest, sent off for the elements of celebration, seeks instead "some poison to kill a pack of rats"; to celebrate his murder, his two brothers consume what he has prepared for him, and his vengeance reaches from beyond the grave.

The Pardoner's degradation of the holiest of Christian sacraments dominates the entire narrative. It begins even before his Prologue and Tale when, invited by Harry Bailey to tell a tale, the Pardoner sarcastically responds with an illusion to bread and wine by demanding drink and "cake," a word commonly used for the consecrated Host: "But first," quod he, "here at this tavern / I will both drink and eat a bit of cake" (*PT*, Introduction, 321–22). The materialization of the Eucharistic sign and its efficacy is achieved through the insistent imagery of gluttonous consumption, which reaches its height in the Pardoner's description of the glutton vomiting up the "red and the white," in which the body of the communicant is figured as a latrine: "Thus of his throat he makes a sewer" (*PT*, 527). Like the image of rats eating the Eucharist, this image of the consumed Host passing through the digestive tract and ending up in a latrine was an obsessive feature of Lollard polemic against the sacrament.

The Pardoner's association of signs with defecation reaches its culmination in his ferocious assault on the miracle of transubstantiation itself:

> Full of dung and of filthy corruption,
> From either end of man, foul is the sound.
> What work, what cost, to feed your appetite!
> These cooks, how they chop, and strain, and grind,
> And transform substance into accident
> All to sate your ravenous appetite. (*PT*, 535–40)

The fact that Chaucer borrowed these lines from the treatise of Lotario dei Segni, *On the Wretchedness of the Human Condition*, greatly increases the richness of the allusion. On the one hand, because Chaucer has the Pardoner use the very words of Cardinal dei Segni, he is automatically associated with him. On the other hand, because the original author employed the extreme imagery of the *contemptu mundi* tradition in order to condemn sensuality, materialism, and literalism, this association is annulled through the Pardoner's boast that he is the very paradigm of these vices, the very ones he preaches against. In this way, he looms as an anti-Lotario dei Segni. The further fact that Chaucer's audience would have known the author of *On the Wretchedness of the Human Condition* not as Cardinal dei Segni but by his later title, Pope Innocent III, introduces into the complexity of the figurative construct associations with the papacy, and thus potentially all of the considerable polemics in fourteenth-century England concerning the papacy, Eucharist, sacraments, and prayer. Through Chaucer's allusion, then, the Pardoner emerges as an anti-papal preacher holding Lollard doctrines.

In the dénouement of his Tale, the Pardoner's horrific contra-transubstantiation of bread and wine into death and perdition completes his assault on signification. Because he fears truth, he ingeniously undermines its vehicle by distorting the meaning of words in his preaching and in his self-presentation. Because he hates life, he deconstructs the authenticity of relics—those traces of the continued life of the dead—and perverts the life-giving sacrament of Communion into a death-dealing consummation.

Just as all of Chaucer's pilgrims in one way or another project themselves into their tales, so, too, does the Pardoner. Some do so unaware, and become the victims of a self-reflexive irony that exposes their shortcomings both as authors and as moral agents. Others, like the Wyf, intentionally represent themselves in one of their characters as a form of wish-fulfillment; the Wyf longs for lost youth and beauty and captures it through the fiction of the

Old Hag's shape-shifting. As we have seen, however, the Wyf unwittingly exposes herself by being to some degree represented in all of her characters.

The Pardoner surely conceives of himself as a member of the young company of "riotours"; all of the sins to which he has confessed in his Prologue are those that he attributes to these characters. Their lusts are his. The alert audience, however, sees in this projection more than the author intended. The brotherhood's quest to find Death reveals the Pardoner himself as a necrophiliac whose degeneracy has left in his soul no room for the love of anything but death.

Moreover, the identification that the Pardoner never intended is the most telling of all. The mysterious old man who points the way to Death for others, cannot, we recall, possess Death himself. Thus he is a sign bereft of the signified: He can "point to" it, but he cannot be one with it. The portrait of the Pardoner throughout the text is of one who, as a materialist, literalist, and relativist has no belief in the truthfulness of the relation between sign and signified, and who continually separates signs from what they are intended to signify. The similitude between the Pardoner's impotency of signification and the incapacity of the old man creates an irresistible identification between them. As the audience perceives more and more clearly through the emergence of the author in his character who signifies death but cannot die, the Pardoner himself is identified as the Living Dead.

11 Canterbury Tales

THE NUN'S PRIEST'S TALE

IT SHOULD NOT be thought, however, that Chaucer depicts all of his pilgrims as gravely flawed morally and intellectually. The Nun's Priest receives no moral censure, and his Tale displays not only brilliant rhetoric but intellectual rectitude, as well. It is the popular mediaeval story of the cock and the fox. Chauntecleer, The Nun's Priest's rooster-hero, resides on the farm of a virtuous, frugal widow, a conventional mediaeval allegory of the widowed Church on earth that cares for the souls left in her protection. Chauntecleer possesses a bevy of glamorous wives—seven, to be exact—of which harem the jewel is Pertelote, an aggressive but beautiful concubine. The plot revolves around Chauntecleer's dream concerning some kind of menace and his debate with Pertelote as to the value of dreams. Rejecting her view that belief in dreams is pure "vanity" and her generally "scientific" approach to the subject, Chauntecleer articulates what might be called the symbolic theory of dreams as signs of truths and prognostications of real events in the world, shoring up his argument with references to Cicero, Macrobius, and other authorities.

Although lighthearted in tone, the development of this traditional beast epic in Chaucer's hands results in a profound examination of a series of philosophical questions as well as a revealing reflection on the nature of allegory, all within the comic mode.

The contrast between the simplicity—indeed, the naïveté—of the story and the complexity of its themes is part of the overall brilliance of the literary achievement. In the course of the narrative, the Nun's Priest addresses not only the question of the efficacy of dreams, but the nature of time, natural knowledge and learned knowledge, the problem of free will and predestination, and, perhaps most significantly, the relation of universals and particulars. All of these questions are handled with a sophisticated mixture of seriousness and irony that lends the Tale its comic-satiric flavor.

The priest who tells the tale is accompanying the Prioress on the pilgrimage. He is a "nun's priest" because he is assigned to the nunnery that the pilgrim Prioress governs; thus he is under her authority. That he tells a story containing a domineering hen and repeated allusions to female treachery suggests that it is his own "henpecked" situation that inspires his storytelling. However, there is far more to the author's use of female figures than subjective resentment: His satire reaches out in many directions and ultimately surpasses itself to become philosophical commentary. We notice this first in the speech he assigns to the tough-minded Pertelote, who, having discovered that it is a dream that causes Chauntecleer's nighttime discomfort and expressions of fear, declares:

> "Oh!" she gasped, "shame on you, lily-liver!"
> "Alas!" she said, "for, by the God above,
> Now have you lost my heart and all my love.
> I cannot love a coward, that's the end!
> For whatever a woman may pretend,
> We all want one thing, if we can it find,
> To have husbands generous, brave and kind,
> And discreet—no misers, nor fools will do,
> Nor him who pales and jumps when he hears 'Boo!' "
> (*Nun's Priest's Tale* [*NPT*], 2908–16)

Now, who does that sound like?

The Nun's Priest, as part of the pilgrim audience, has heard the Wyf of Bath pontificating on "what all women want," and he transports her controversial opinions into the mouth of his fictional hen. Like the Wyf, who loved best her fifth, dominant husband because he was manly and wouldn't give in to her, Pertelote, too, feels authorized to announce what all women want. This device of having a fictional character reflect one or more of the pilgrims extends the range of allusion from the domineering hen to the Prioress and further to the Wyf of Bath, and the allusion is satirical.

But this is not the end of the author's extension; he now grounds all of the female allusions in the typological figure from Genesis:

> "I counsel you the best—I do not lie—
> . . . .
> All about herbs I shall myself you teach
> That shall be for your health and for your leech."
> (*NPT*, 2945, 2949–50)

Now who does that sound like?

It has been said that what Pertelote wanted to feed Chauntecleer—a concoction of laurel, hellebore, euphorbia, and several other herbs—would have been fatal. Everyone in the Nun's Priest's audience, including us, recalls the woman who advised her husband to eat something that led to deadly consequences; with this allegorical identification of Eve, the satirical extension is complete: Pertelote is an Eve figure whose similarity to the Prioress and the Wyf makes of them metaphorical Eves as well.

But *The Nun's Priest's Tale* is not a full-blown allegory, for as soon as we get hold of the allegorical clue (Pertelote signifies Eve), the author seems to annul it and move on to play with other literary models. In a truly typological tale based on the Fall, Chauntecleer-as-Adam would eat what Pertelote-as-Eve proffers; but he doesn't. Instead, the author throws into doubt the cause of his hero's "fall," and depicts him, unlike Adam, not only rejecting his wife's advice, but ignoring as well the warning in the dream he has just had:

> "Let us stop this debate and speak more fair.
> Madame Pertelote, I do declare,
> God has surely given me greatest grace;
> For when I see the beauty of your face,
> So bright be the red around your eyes,
> That all my caution—away it flies.
> How true the saying, '*In principio,*
> *Mulier est hominis confusio*'—
> Madame, the meaning of this Latin is,
> 'Woman is man's joy and all his bliss!'" (*NPT*, 3157–65)

With Chauntecleer's magisterial citation of Latin and his mis-translation of it, the Nun's Priest further extends the trope of the Fall and simultaneously introduces still another theme: the meaning of words. The Latin phrase states a popular aphorism, that "in the beginning (of the world), a woman caused the fall of man," exactly the opposite of Chauntecleer's translation. Adam's error was, of course, to have behaved as if his woman were the fullness of his happiness. ("Was she thy God that thou obeyest her?" as Milton put it.)[1] Beyond theological considerations, however, the mistranslation raises the question of whether words have meaning in and of themselves or whether they can mean what we want them to. Obviously for Chauntecleer, the meaning of these words is determined by desire, for having proclaimed his translation, he flies down from his perch in pursuit of his sensual bliss and "treads" his hen as many as twenty times.

The epistemological theme has, in fact, started earlier in the Tale with the author's initial description of the hero, who, we are told, possessed "natural knowledge" that allowed him to sound the hour with his crowing more accurately than the town clock. Added to this way of knowing is the intellectual understanding that Chauntecleer pretends to in his interpretation of the symbolism of his dream. His description of his dream is highly significant:

---

[1] John Milton, *Paradise Lost,* book 9, stanza 10.

> I dreamt that I was strutting up and down
> Within our yard, when I perceived a beast,
> Like a hound, and it wanted to seize me,
> Snatch my body and maul me to death.
> His color was between yellow and red,
> And tipped was his tail and both of his ears
> With black, unlike the rest of his body;
> His snout was small, his two eyes were glowing. (*NPT*, 2898–905)

Later, at the moment when the fox actually appears in the yard, the Nun's Priest comments that an animal will flee an enemy, "Even though, he never before saw it" (*NPT*, 3281). As these passages reveal, Chauntecleer has no previous experience of foxes before encountering one in his dream, nor is he able to give a name to that which he sees in his dream and describes. Yet he has true knowledge of the nature of the fox and rightly fears it. How is this possible?

What the dreamer encounters in his dream is not a particular fox, but the universal fox, or foxness, which he understands through the various characteristics, or "accidents" as they were called in the Middle Ages, such as color and shape. Chauntecleer does not need a name in order to understand the reality of the universal he dreams, nor, even when he encounters a particular fox in the yard, does he need to name it in order to know it and fear it. The way the author manages the scene establishes a number of things: that not all dreams arise, as Pertelote would have it, from subjective causes; that there is a reality beyond the subjective and that it can communicate with us; and, most important, particulars do not precede universals. Furthermore, universals, such as foxness, exist independent of any experience of their particular manifestations. The fact that Chauntecleer apparently never learns the word "fox," but learns all he has to know about foxes, also points to the fact that universals are not mere words for abstracted experiences.

Forewarned by a prophetic dream and armed with a knowledge of the danger, Chauntecleer nevertheless falls. There are certain subtle theological queries implied here: Did Chauntecleer fall because he took his wife's advice? If not, can we look back at the earlier analogy and ask: Did Adam fall because he took Eve's advice, or, like Chauntecleer, because of an act of personal pride?

Another question arises and is made explicit by the Nun's Priest: Was the rooster preordained to fall, and no matter how many warnings he might have had, fate was bound to prove stronger? The philosophical debate over free will and determinism was a hot topic in Chaucer's time, and it was one heavily influenced by theology. In the discussion of God's attributes, His omniscience is primary in this debate: If God is all-knowing and His knowledge is perfect, He knows that I will be saved or damned. How is it possible, then, that human beings have free will whilst God knows their destiny in such a way that it cannot be otherwise?

The determinist concludes that I have no free will with which to earn my own salvation, and would take the experience of Chauntecleer as demonstrating just that. But knowledge alone is insufficient for salvation. Warned by instinct and his dream, Chauntecleer nevertheless "falls." Significantly, the cause of his fall is specified as pride excited by the flattery of the fox. The fox's sweet words overcome the rooster's natural knowledge, and we realize that the Nun's Priest's message concerning language is that as long as words are signs, they can be made to stand for things other than their proper signifieds. Thus lies are possible. By the same token, the very existence of the lie attests to the existence of the truth that the lie requires to be a lie.

Describing to Chauntecleer how magnificently his "father" sang, by closing his eyes, stretching his neck, and crowing forth, the fox muses that Chauntecleer's song is probably even more beautiful. "Lets see," he says, "whether you can *imitate* your father "(*NPT*, 3321, my emphasis). Thus the Nun's Priest steers the narrative back to the allegory of the Fall and its consequences in which all mankind imitates his father, Adam, through a personal fall.

Although Chauntecleer falls through pride and concupiscence, redemption is possible. Just as humanity lost its natural innocence and natural understanding through the subtlety of the Enemy, so Chauntecleer's natural knowledge fails him—or, rather, he ignores it. But just as mankind uses the fallen language of his post-lapsarian existence to reconstruct his lost innocence and communication with God, so Chauntecleer, having learned how fallen language works, can use it to save himself through his own use of ambiguity and hidden intention:

> In all his fear unto the fox he spoke,
> And said to him, "Sir, if I were you,
> I would yell at them who are chasing you,
> 'Turn back all of you, you good-for-nothings!
> May a pestilence descend upon you!
> Now that I am come to the forest's edge,
> The cock stays where he is, despite you all,
> And by my faith, I will eat him whole.'" (*NPT*, 3407–17)

Tempted by pride, the fox takes his captive's advice, and as he opens his mouth to defy the rescuers, Chauntecleer flies to the top of a tree. The fox's second attempt to deceive him with honey-eyed words fails, for, having learned the nature of fallen language, Chauntecleer uses it for his own restitution:

> No you don't! Shame on you and shame on me,
> But if you fool me twice, my shame is worse. (*NPT*, 3426–27)

The Nun's Priest's Tale, as we have seen, picks up and weaves together threads from many of the tales that precede it. The whole fabric of the Tale offers a commentary on a range of philosophical topics, bits and pieces of which are found in the other pilgrims' tales where they are, more often than not treated erroneously or even deceptively. Our naïve Narrator has by and large been an undependable guide to the truth that lies in fiction; he seems delighted by the Wyf of Bath's good humor, but fails to see the faultiness of her exegesis or her pathetic confusion about the nature of time and aging. He is repelled by the Pardoner but can offer no rebuttal to his nominalistic relativism.

Chaucer, the great master of irony, apparently felt the need to set the record straight, and it would seem he did so in two ways. He speaks straightforwardly in the so-called *Retraction* at the end of the *Canterbury Tales*, where he apologizes for any aesthetic or philosophical failures of his poetry, and then, as if to be sure we realize that his subtle irony has been put aside, Chaucer states clearly his authorial intention and links it to St. Paul:

> For our Book declares "all that is written
> Is so written for our understanding."
> And that is my intention. (*Retraction* [R] 1078–79)

The Nun's Priest's Tale is the other way Chaucer makes clear the proper perspective on these matters. In it he conspicuously links the contents of this tale to his own statements in the *Retraction* by having the Nun's Priest anticipate him by citing the same passage from St. Paul at the end of his tale:

> But for you who think this tale is silly
> That it's about a cock, a fox, a hen,
> Seize the morality in it, good men.
> For Saint Paul says that all that written is,
> For our understanding it written is. (*NPT*, 3438–42)

CONCLUSION

ST. PAUL EXPLAINS his statement that whatsoever is written is for our understanding by adding "so that by patience and through the consolation of Scripture, we may have hope" (Romans 15:4). A consolation is needed because of the fallen human condition and the fallen state of language, which is its consequence. Paul seems to be saying somewhat paradoxically that language itself is the consolation that, with patience, leads to overcoming the Fall, and, thus language, written and spoken, is its own consolation, for it has within it the power of redemption.

The understanding of the drama of language in the Middle Ages was drawn, like so many other concepts, from biblical exegesis. The centrality of language is immediately signaled in Genesis by the fact that the Judeo–Christian God creates through language, "speaking" into existence all that exists. That God shares this creative gift with humanity is seen in the description of Adam's naming of the animals (Genesis 2:19–20). The fact that "whatsoever Adam called every living creature, that was the name thereof" indicates that he possesses a share of the creative power in which the sign and the signified are one, for he perceives the very essence of each animal and so can recognize its natural and essential name. Just as in Eden there is a perfect unity between the sign and the signified in which the animal is its name and the name is the animal, so, too, there is the same perfect unity between man and woman. Adam rightly declares, "This now is bone of my bones, flesh of my flesh" (Genesis 2:23). All of this reflects the unity between man and God who possess such easy communication that God regularly walks with the first pair in the Garden, conversing with them.

The Fall of mankind is chiefly characterized by the loss of unity and the discovery of difference that we see as the immediate effects of eating the forbidden fruit: Adam and Eve become aware of their difference and are ashamed ("They knew that they were naked," Genesis 3:7). Their new self-consciousness leads them to hide from God (Genesis 3:8), and finally to turn against each other (Genesis 3:12–13).

In being based on difference, postlapsarian language is no longer God-like, and along with all the other disunities introduced into the world, the divorce of sign and signified occurs. The fall of language is completed with the building and destruction of the tower of Babel, which represents the desire of man to be God and to name himself, to self-author, and to be one's own authority: "Let us make us a name" (Genesis 11:4), which is but the expression of the intention to make words subservient to desire and to impose upon language the shape of the human will.

After the Fall, the human quest becomes one to reconstruct the lost unity, to restore the communication between God and man, the harmony between man and woman, and the union between sign and signified. Throughout history there have been brief glimpses of this reunion. The Hebrew Prophets communicated God's message to His people; through marriage man and woman attain mutual harmony, however imperfect; and through the gift of poetry sign and signified, word and thing, verge on oneness.

At last, the entry of the Divinity Himself into the world as the Word of God signals the simultaneous redemption of humanity and of language. That Jesus is known as the *Verbum Dei* deepens the linguistic sense of God's nature already revealed in His speaking the world into existence in Genesis. The Incarnation reunites words with the Word and provides the authority and power to signify truth.

The vocation of every poet—every author—is to realize this power of words by using them so as to incarnate the truths into which his understanding and spirit have penetrated, and to raise language up, as it were, so as to be adequate to this insight. In the canon of English literature, Geoffrey Chaucer is among the first in a long line of poets to bring about this incarnation and to infuse words with a life that, after 600 years, still uplifts language and, however briefly, buys back its faults.

INDEX